GOVERNMENT
AGAINST
THE PEOPLE

The Economics of Political Exploitation

Rodney Atkinson

Comments on individual essays by

Milton Friedman, Mancur Olson
and David Howell

Published by
Compuprint Publishing
4 Sands Road
Swalwell Industrial Estate
Tyne and Wear NE16 3DJ
Tel: 091 488 8936

Copyright © Compuprint Publishing 1986

ISBN 0 9509353 1 X

Price: £9.00

Cover design by Jaine MacCormack
Typesetting by Auckland Vidiset Ltd
12 Greenland St, London NW1 0ND.
Tel: 01-482 2757

Printed and bound in Great Britain at
The Camelot Press Ltd, Southampton

Contents

Preface

The essays in this book are a highly critical analysis of Government, not of particular Governments. The analysis and prescriptions do not sit easily with any of the major political parties in the United Kingdom and cannot be categorised simply in terms of the outdated "Left-Right" political axis.

The author is concerned with the gross discrepancy between the theory of Democracy as the expression of the people's will and the practice of "Democratic Government" which has been based on the contradiction of that will. Periodic elections alone provide no obvious remedy to this subtle erosion of democracy. A change of political hand at the levers of State control does nothing to reduce the number of those levers. The Establishments of Left and Right – so brilliantly combined in post war corporatism – are increasingly seen as two forms of the same authoritarianism. The "centre" parties, ostensibly placed between these pseudo opposites, have largely failed to recognise the strong libertarian mood of the electorate. Despite qualified conversions to market economics and the acceptance of political decentralisation, many of their prescriptions have all the hallmarks of the corporatism which the people reject. Their acceptance of nationalised monopolies, their rejection of, for instance, education vouchers and their miriad "organising" committees are the very lifeblood of State paternalism and represent the emasculation of public choice democracy.

It is a sad reflection on the "liberal" parties that it has been a Conservative Government which has most effectively espoused radical liberalism. It is Mrs Thatcher – often despite the traditions of her own party – who has reduced the power of producers and re-established the sovereignty of consumers, thereby simultaneously re-establishing the power of voters and decreasing the power of non-elected interest groups.

1

To what extent have other politicians recognised the conflict between Government power and democratic public choice? To what extent are they prepared to reduce further the role of Government (and the "importance" of their own positions) and grant more freedom and responsibility to a populace eager and able to accept them?

For those politicians who still claim that the first step in the people's salvation is the Government's intervention, the sad tale of Government failure detailed in these pages may induce a long overdue modesty.

The Author

Rodney Atkinson was born in Gosforth Northumberland in 1948. He has an Honours degree from the University of Newcastle upon Tyne and a Master of Science from Durham University. He is a member of the Institute of Linguists. He formerly lectured at the University of Mainz, West Germany before returning to England to take up senior managerial posts, firstly at Grindlays Bank, then at Banque Paribas in London. He now divides his time between family business management in Northumberland and writing and financial consultancy in London. He has advised Ministers at the Department of Energy and the Treasury and has advised the House of Commons Select Committee on Energy. His articles have appeared in, among others, The Times, Financial Times and Guardian and he has commented on economic affairs on radio and television.

Tables and Statistics

Definitions

The author has coined the following terms. They are used in the essays indicated.

TAXPLOITATION

Is the process whereby, because of Government action or inaction, a windfall or monopoly profit accrues to a producer and Government joins in the exploitation of the consumer by maintaining the circumstances which provide the excess profit and then taxing it. (Taxploitation).

THE YOYO EFFECT

Is the relationship between a given change in industrial countries' GDP and the resulting magnified change in LDC export growth. The effect is greatest and most destabilising when industrial economies fluctuate from recession to inflationary boom. (A safer road for Young Nation debtors).

ALIENATION OF CAPITAL

As profitability falls and inflation rises direct investment in companies and Government Stock declines. Investors turn increasingly to short term *bank* deposits while corporations and Governments turn to bank loans. Banks, instead of fulfilling their role as providers of short term *finance* become long term *investors* but only as intermediaries between the depositors and the debtors. This alienates the investor from his investment and the owner from his capital. (A safer road for Young Nation debtors).

THE WRONG CONSENSUS

Is Government based on the accommodation (usually disguised by the process of inflation) of the demands of those unelected groups powerful enough to threaten or influence Government. The Wrong Consensus can only arise where Government oversteps the bounds of its legitimate role as provider of "public goods". (The Moral Basis of Monetarism).

Introduction

If there has been a common element in the decline of western industrial economies and the instability of international finance it has been the inexorable rise in the direct power of the State over the people.

Government took into "public" ownership companies and whole industries, raised taxes and used the proceeds to purchase votes and to direct investment into the most futile and wasteful projects. The vast apparatus of the welfare State, sold to voters as the protector of the weak, sporned armies of poorly qualified middle class administrators with comfortable salaries and offices while the intended recipients of this largesse were frustrated by bureaucratic muddle and then taxed almost to the level of their benefits.

When the spending of Government could not be financed honestly through taxation Government used inflation to relieve the people of their savings. When the services of State owned industries were not purchased by free consumers, the people through their taxes were forced to pay for them whether they consumed them or not. When the people needed houses and education the State provided tower blocks and illiteracy. When the people wished to work, the State-backed closed shop excluded them. When the people wished to buy superior foreign goods the State limited their import, raising the prices and profits of domestic producers. When the people wanted more coal, doctors or television channels the State helped those industries to restrict the number of producers, hence driving up the price of their services. When the people required more skilled workers the State gave Trade Unions the power to restrict the number of such workers and make unskilled work more remunerative. When the developing countries wished to trade freely industrial country Governments protected their markets (quietly and unobtrusively) and then (with much trumpet blowing and claims to compassion) gave aid in recompense.

What then of the concept of Democracy – that widely available placebo to calm the protestations of the people who see no convergence between the will of the electorate and the interests of those who govern? How can it now be so evident that Government and its extensive power structure has interests – economic and political – which are often diametrically opposed to those of the people?

Legitimate Government is the extension of the will of the people to those activities which the people acting in free association could not perform without Government. Not that the definition of such Government activity is universal and unchanging. Many so called "public goods" can become "private goods" as technology advances and wealth and education increase. For instance for many years the public radio and television network – BBC, and the public telephone network were indeed public goods. But now advanced technology allows many producers to service and charge individual consumers without the intervention of the State. For many years it was not technically possible to measure the amounts of gas or electricity passing into and out of a gas pipeline or electricity grid with sufficient accuracy. Now this is possible many suppliers can supply many consumers using the grids as "common carrier". There is therefore no need for a State gas or electricity company.

There are of course public goods aspects to many commercial activities. It is doubtful whether the privately run railways would have been so successful in Victorian England had Government not passed laws to facilitate the construction of track across the land of thousands of individual owners. Similarly it is unlikely that corporations in industrial towns or coal fire owners in London would have spontaneously and successfully reduced their noxious emissions had it not been for Government laws and monitoring of those emissions.

However Government has not restricted its activities to provision of public goods. The overriding power which the people delegated to Government for *specific* purposes became too attractive to be used so sparingly. Government overstepped the bounds of its legitimate role as an extension of the people's will and began to raise revenue not to complement the people's decisions but to override and contradict them. Government became an owner of industry, an intervener in commercial activity, the setter and controler of prices, the controler of savings and most important of all the dispenser of money and favours. Corruption always starts with those administering the source of power – politicians and civil servants. There is a wide range of rewards which can only be distributed by Government – inflation proof salaries and pensions, important posts in the "public service", knighthoods, peerages and a plethora of lesser honours, waivers and immunities from laws, special allowances against taxation etc. At this stage we begin to see the advantage for groups outside Government spending much time and money lobbying the central political power so that some of these privileges can be more appropriately distributed! Not surprisingly assiduous lobbying does bear fruit and more and more individuals, corporations and institutions decide that time spent in Westminister and Whitehall is more enjoyable and profitable than serving the people in a competitive market.

Government itself, in the shape of nationalised industries, need not even go to such trouble. As the owner of assets, monopoly supplier, law maker, protector from the inconvenience of foreign competition and regulator of safety and pollution it has no need to worry about any challenge to its irresponsible hegemony.

Needless to say it is the user of State run railways and air services who see overpriced services decline, not the consumer of clothes, food or computers provided by the competitive market. It is the British Steel Corporation, British Nuclear Fuels and Electricity Generating Board – all State run, who are the greatest polluters of the environment. It was the insanitary conditions in the kitchens of State run hospitals which could not be remedied because of "crown immunity" to prosecution. Any commercial enterprise with similar conditions, said the Government's own inspectorate, would have been prosecuted and closed.

The only guarantee a Government can give is that the people will be paying for that guarantee. When Government owns commercial assets the people, as captive consumers, no longer have any control over their use. Indeed the people even lose the vital role of Government as regulator. Government as both offender and regulator will not use its powers to protect the environment or enforce the laws when that threatens their own commercial interests. If Government has *interests* then those who govern will always contradict the democratic will.

Government is a legal entity, constitutionally separate from those who vote for it, the people. The relationship is not dissimilar to that between shareholder and limited company.

8

However in commercial life the company cannot have interests independent of the shareholders since the shareholders *are* the company. They have a common commerčial interest. In theory there should be a similar identity between people and Government, the legal and constitutional distinction being merely a technical vehicle for collective action, not a division between competing interests. However, whereas limited companies must compete with other commercial producers to serve free consumers under a rule of law, Governments have overriding and unchallengeable power in every sphere of social life where it chooses to intervene. Government therefore rapidly takes on a distinct and separate set of interests from those of the people. Whereas individuals and corporations benefit only if they serve their fellow citizens, Government and its acolytes can benefit by exploiting them and using the full panoply of State power to disguise the fact.

The distinctive characteristic of collectivist or State coercion is its *covert* nature. Nothing is open to scrutiny. Costs, prices and profits are not impersonally determined by the market – they are controled by the State. They cease to be signals of facts for all to see and become part of the smokescreen constructed by those in power. Rewards for individuals and corporations cease to be open as gross salaries and profits subject to a universal tax and come instead in the form of tax free benefits or income taxed at many different rates according to the array of "special allowances" which each industrial interest group has obtained from Government. While posts in the commercial sector are openly advertised, Government has a covert "muggins turn" approach for many public sector appointments and others are used as blatant rewards for political colleagues. The large discrepancy between general tax rates and the actual tax paid by those with special allowances has an equivalent in the law where Government, Nationalised Industries and Trade Unions are all granted immunities to laws which apply to the people in general.

Such covert exploitation of the people by Government is now so extensive that many are at last becoming aware of the lack of identity between Government and people. Everyday frustrations at the cost and inefficiency of public service, high tax levels, public corruption, the waste of public "enterprise" and the blatant discrepancy between individual knowledge and collective ignorance to eventually penetrate the public consciousness. Nevertheless by far the greatest majority of

9

Government failures are effectively disguised and so long as Government has absolute power (in the United Kingdom there is not even the constraint of a written Constitution) the freedom of the people to *fully* expose the inadequacies of Government is severely restricted.

The democratic vote is an opportunity for the people to stand back from the responsible pursuit of their rational self interest and judge "the whole". It is not easy to sum the daily frustrations of individual, family and corporate existence into a definitive statement about the proper role of Government, not least because Government is adept at disguising their involvement in our lives and equally adept at avoiding the consequences of having done so.

This collection of essays is an attempt to expose the nature of Government's contradiction of the people's will and to demonstrate how, far from being a protective and benign influence Government has become a powerful, self interested and parasitic burden on those it purports to represent. The essays are divided into three sections. Part 1 covers prices, incomes, inflation and the monetarist cure. Inflation – the failure to preserve the value of the people's currency and savings – is one of the very few tasks which Government *might* have been able to perform – at least it had slightly more legitimacy than the detailed intervention in and ownership of business described in Part II. But as in many other "public good" roles of Government their failure has been grotesque, long lasting and relatively unchallenged.

Part II shows how intervention to create that which Government and its publicly financed economists deem to be beneficial in fact brought about the very opposite of what they intended. The chapters on international aid, trade and debt show how these disastrous policies of the industrial countries have been transported via international financial instability and inter Governmental "remedies" to the poorest countries. If there were free trade in ideas those offered by western developed countries would have been purchased by no one. Unfortunately the power of trade block protectionism and internationally administered finance (IMF, World Bank) and trade (GATT) is so great that the "North" is able to impose on the developing world not only its economic failure but also its State interventionism as a "solution" to that failure.

Part III is a series of "mini case studies" of Government exploitation of the people they purport to represent. The studies are divided into 3 categories – "Taxploitation", The Failure of Public Enterprise and the Failure of Public Goods. It is a sad catalogue of ineptitude rather than the result of malice. Not that the motivation is of much relevance to a people suffering Government "protection".

Part IV is an attempt to define Democracy, not just in its rather limited form of Parliamentary representation but also in its more potent and direct form of *public choice democracy*. Quis custodiet ipsos custodes? In the end the only solution to the control of the State is the freedom of the people to choose – but that may threaten some very comfortable not to say profitable myths about Democracy!

PART I

The Politics of Inflation and Monetarism

1 Inflation and Middle Class Values

Inflation is the symptom of Government accommodation of those elements in society which resort to collectivist coercion of political institutions, in order to obtain the rewards which they have failed to obtain by their ability or skill. The inflationary process is directly destructive of four 'middle class' values: self-reliance, thrift, education and the Rule of Law. These values are of course the basis of any democratic society, and the stability and justice of society will depend on their preservation. Over recent decades, we have witnessed the erosion of these values and their gradual replacement by the rule of naked power. Such power was not open to challenge by those who questioned it politically, nor by those who could have exposed and dissipated it commercially.

Government was persuaded by powerful interest groups – partly through the carrot of patronage, partly through the stick of coercion – that laws should be enacted to widen those groups' legal immunities, to increase their fiscal exemptions, or to prevent the embarassment of commercial competition. Government duly obliged and in so doing itself grew in size and power until its bureaucratic tentacles and collectivist patronage destroyed both political accountability and individual responsibility. Once the commercial and entrepreneurial avenues to the service of society were effectively blocked, there remained only one way for the able to influence events, even in their own environment, and that was to organise and agitate at a sufficient intensity and volume. Only thus could they turn the grinding wheels of Whitehall in their direction. A premium was paid not for skill, knowledge, training, business acumen or community

12

service but for verbal agility, leaflet distribution, committee nobbling, hand pumping, cocktail drinking and vote buying. Galbraith thought the sign of a decadent society was the cream of the country's graduates employed in detergent advertising, but it is far worse to see that ability locked into a perpetual dialogue with political bureaucracy. It is easier to avoid detergent than pervasive Government.

Neither the political route to economic power nor the economic purchase of political power find any support in the values of the middle class – nor for that matter in middle class values. Let us be clear that it is middle class *values,* and not the middle classes themselves, which have been the bastion of social stability. Those values have to a large extent been shared by all classes, while many of those who have contributed to their erosion have been members of the middle class.

While the son of a miner has valued training, thrift and monetary rewards for commercial success, the son of the doctor or teacher has often abandoned his university studies, enjoyed impecunious 'freedom', and despised the successful entrepreneur from a more lowly background than himself. Even at the height of the resentment and deprecation of middle class values in the 60s and 70s, when the most cynical descriptions of those values came from the plum-filled mouths of the home counties media, there were many working class sons and daughters (mercifully screened from such influences) who invested in training and education. Today they garner the fruits of that work in the form of semi-detached responsibility. Their offspring will in turn either succumb to a repetition of anti-middle class sentiment and waste what their parents have built, or resist the pseudo-intellectual blandishments of social iconoclasts, and consolidate their family's educational and financial fortunes, for the benefit of future generations.

Middle class values include the sense of a national identity, and the reliance on parliamentary representation to provide the overall cohesion and social discipline of a Rule of Law. They also include an implicit faith in the family, as the indispensible forum of personal love and personal responsibility. Over recent years the family has been exposed to great social, economic and political pressure. Economic success has provided the individual wealth for offspring to establish their own separate 'single' existences. Shifting moral standards have encouraged a duty-free attitude to personal relationships. Collectivist values, which have been set against those of the family, are fantasies, dreams of a world from which true individual responsibility has been eliminated.

The most significant casualty of collectivist thinking has been the sacrifice of personal and family responsibility to the assumed protective qualities of the state. Naturally this attitude has permeated most corporations and institutions who ceased to accept their responsibilities or to take any pride in their achievements. They preferred to demand their rights, to look to government for guarantees and to define their responsibilities within narrow limits, assuming their commercial failure to be the fault of others. The Government's accommodation of these demands has involved the debasement of the political currency. The state's self-image as the eternal provider grew in importance, as the willingness of the people to pay for state-distributed largesse declined. The fall in the value of money was a direct attack on capital by consumers and led by a Government, which increasingly represented, not the creative forces which sutain society but the irresponsible elements which merely depend upon it. This constituted a slow, undetectable, pernicious attack on another middle class value – thrift.

Savings are not only the fruits of labour, they are an investment in the provision of future wealth and income. The most vulnerable forms of saving are bank and building society deposits and Government 'gilt edged' stock. Such investments are typical among the young, the poor and the old – those who are themselves the most vulnerable members of society. All have paid a bitter price as inflation has raided their savings.

Most trade unions also deal in money investments: they are called wage agreements. Unions negotiate a contract defined in terms of pounds per week, the real value of which is progressively devalued by inflation. Strong unions break their agreements with impunity while weaker unions are forced to deal in devalued currency. Inflation exploits the weak who hold to agreements, and rewards the strong for breaking them. So falls another middle class value – the integrity of contract – and with it the Rule of Law itself.

What of the principal route to economic and social advancement, education? Educational values suffered in two ways. Firstly the self doubt of educationalists about the disciplined structure of learning, and the increasing inadequacy of teaching staff, allowed a generation of children to leave school without even basic literate and numerical skills. Secondly the power of mass trade unionism was able to achieve higher rewards for mere muscle than for the years of disciplined apprenticeship and university study. This in turn led to shortages of skills, to bankruptcy, and to high unemployment, and so to a declining remuneration for educational achievement. The good in learning was neither defined by the schools nor supported by society – so it was driven out by the bad.

The reversal of so many of these shameful defeats for middle class values has now begun. Lower inflation preserves the value of thrift and self reliance. The Rule of Law protects those who are trustworthy and punishes the arbitrary rule of naked power. A healthy market economy prevents the maintenance of privilege by the politically powerful. A consistent currency of educational standards allows teachers to define their responsibilities, while permitting the less advantaged to challenge for any job in society. The reduction in the power of the state, its patronage and its subsidies releases resources for responsible use by individuals and corporations, the arbiters being competition and public choice.

Middle class values are once more esteemed. They will best serve, not the middle class, but those who aspire to their success, knowing that such success must be individually earned not granted by the patronage of a bureaucracy answerable only to powerful interest groups.

2   Incomes Policies Do Not Work (The Inflation Tax)

The discussion of the SDP's 'inflation tax' presents an opportunity to analyse many political assumptions about 'inflation', the reasons for economic decline and what politicians are prepared to undertake to reverse it. The 'guru' of the 'inflation tax', Professor Richard Layard of the London School of Economics has proposed an inflation tax which is palatable enough for an ambitious politician to swallow; but in producing such a saccharine package of 'sensible moderation' Layard has sacrificed the economic honesty and unwelcome historical evidence which would indicate far harder and more honest remedies.

Layard's inflation tax starts from the assumption that we have to 'control' prices and in particular the price of labour. The central role of wages in this understanding of inflation finds expression in the ubiquitous concept of 'wage inflation'. But there is no such thing as wage inflation any more than there is 'oil inflation' or 'jelly baby inflation'. This confusion is at the heart of all non-monetarist attempts to tackle the UK's economic problems. Inflation is not an attribute of a commodity but of money itself. It is nothing other than the debasement of the currency brought about by excessive borrowing through the banking system to finance that which cannot be funded honestly. Since only the market-immune central and local government and nationalised industries are ever in a position to borrow excessively (commercial companies, *pace* Laker, cannot borrow more than prudent bankers will allow) and only they do not have to worry about a satisfactory return on the investment of such borrowed funds, it is here that we find the root causes of inflation. The inflation tax, however, will not and indeed cannot effectively penalise the public sector institutions which are the prime instigators of inflation.

Layard's inflation tax is, at least, a small advance on the old ideas of incomes policy, but unlike an incomes policy, which at least confronted the power of trade unions, the inflation tax seeks to influence the trade union bargainers indirectly by penalising the employer. The assumption is that it is the employer paying his workers too much who must be taught a

16

lesson. Layard arrives at this conclusion even though he starts by admitting that it is monopoly *union* power which forces us to accept this form of incomes control. The inflation tax seeks to influence workers by penalising the company for which they work in the hope that this will affect wage settlements. But if workers will not act responsibly in the face of the disciplines of the market place, they will certainly not do so if the discipline comes in the form of a politically inspired tax. However, where market disciplines operate there is really little evidence that trade unions are irresponsible. Excessive wage settlements have occurred principally in those areas of the *non*-market public sector where there is monopoly and payment for the excess is extracted from consumer or taxpayer. But what sanction can a tax be for a Government or nationalised industry? The concept of the inflation tax completely avoids the important questions of the efficient and responsible use of national resources. Instead it attempts to tackle a *symptom* of national malaise – inflation.

This form of incomes policy would be permanent. Firms which increase the average earnings of their workers above the Government norm (can we imagine unions settling below the Government approved norm?) will always be penalised, regardless of any wish to allow their employees to share in increased profits. Layard admits that, since the norm will apply to rises in average earnings, there will be an incentive to employ relatively more unskilled labour. This he describes as a 'mild distortion'. In a country chronically short of skilled workers, with one of the worst records for training, retraining and job mobility, Layard constructs a system of incentives to perpetuate our incompetence. It is also admitted that there would be plenty of scope for employers to cheat. This is accepted on the grounds that there is already scope for cheating with National Insurance and PAYE payments. Layard thus proposes to widen the number of tax payment systems which could involve cheating! It is further admitted that because companies will not be able to attract new labour as they expand, it will 'slow down the redeployment of labour'. But this is deemed to create employment. By saddling all industrial assets with the burden of either labour shortages or over-supply, Layard's proposal is even worse than a Government job creation scheme.

For administrative reasons only major employers can be included. Smaller firms, therefore, will be free to do what they like. There will exist an artificial bias towards firms outside the scheme which will recruit the most able and skilled workers who cannot obtain their market price in the controlled sector. Indeed there will be an incentive among companies in the controlled sector to rid themselves of their most able workers. If small is more efficient let the market tell us, not Professor Layard.

The administration of the tax will be costly. The authorities will be as powerless as under conventional incomes policies to control abuses. The inflation tax does not even fulfil the simple conditions of definition as a 'tax' since no Government revenue will be raised. Any sums taxed away from companies who have paid their workers too much will be repaid to the whole of the corporate sector in the form of reductions in National Insurance contributions.

Every year there would be a change in the corporate NI rate as the inflation tax-take fluctuated. Since an adjustment could be made only once a year there would always be a temporarily increased tax burden until it was refunded during the following year. If all companies exceeded the pay rise norm by the same amount (let us say, paid the going rate), the penalty to all companies would be nil, since refunds through National Insurance contributions are to be equal to the tax raised. By taking the year-on-year average rise in earnings of a company's workforce there would be immense distortions where a large number of employees were on commission and – as is usual – where there was a big change in business activity over the period. What would happen if a strike had affected the previous year's earnings? There would be a penalty for a company which did not have an equally damaging strike during the current year.

Real conflict with Government could arise where a strong trade union demands a rise, say, 2% above the norm, but which the company could afford. The extra imposition of the 'inflation tax' on the company could bankrupt it. What does the Government do? The workers would see Government for the first time as their opponent and not the company.

The basic assumption behind the inflation tax is that the scope for economic growth (and hence, it is assumed, more jobs) depends on suppressing wages below what they would otherwise be to 'leave room' for growth. Total employment, however, even in the short term and certainly in the long term, does not depend on aggregate demand but on the efficiency of the pricing system in signalling the relative supply of and demand for individual commodities and various kinds of labour. It is the failure to do this that results in pressures on Government to 'expand demand' by devaluing money which in turn exacerbates the underlying failure in the real economy.

If Professor Layard rightly sees macro-economic monetarism as inadequate, we can praise his attempts to curb excessive wage rises *only if his scheme promotes micro-economic efficiency.* Although he recognises the importance, and has seen the distorting effects, of traditional wages policies, he has developed an 'inflation tax' which avoids tackling the real balance of power in the economy. It will not prevent the government from promoting inflation, and it introduces further incentives for market distortion. In the end it is an attempt to control a symptom because tackling a cause would be politically unacceptable. But that is precisely the story of the last 30 years.

3 Inflation and the Oil Price

When Governments intervene in the market place to bring about a situation they want or to suppress a situation they dislike they contradict, in effect, what the market mechanism is indicating is the truth. The resources Governments need to achieve this are immense and the cost to the fiscal purse embarassing. In addition the cost to the people in the form of artificial pricing, under-supply or suppressed costs are considerable. Because those whom Government claims it is protecting are not prepared to pay these overt costs Government has a covert remedy to hand – it creates more money. This has three convenient effects – it gives Government more spending power, it takes money from the people's savings without their knowledge and it disguises the true cost of Government failure.

This was the process used by Governments during the 1960's and 1970's to disguise the chronic decline in economic efficiency in western economies. The Americans led the way and set in train the inflationary process which not only misled Americans but also conveniently misled foreign exporters to the USA about the value of the Dollars exchanged for their exports. Chief among these were oil producing countries who were in fact paid Dollars, regardless to which country they exported.

At first oil exporters suffered lower real Dollar prices as US inflation responded to artificial money demand but then once they realised the power of their cartel they took advantage of that very demand to force prices up. They did not *control* the price – as subsequent oil price falls proved – but they could *take advantage* of high demand as long as it lasted.

Table 1 demonstrates these two phases. From 1965 to 1974 falling real US interest rates indicate the increasingly inflationary environment. From 1970 to 1974 OPEC producers were able to achieve a quadrupling of the oil price, not because production fell but because demand rose sharply. During the years of recession 1974-1975 OECD real growth and real and nominal interest rates fell so that oil demand was insufficient to sustain OPEC power.

Physical supply and demand for any commodity are to the greatest extent dependent on price adjustment. In modern economies the price of commodities is in turn to the greatest

20

extent dependent on the real price of money, namely interest rates.

Interest rates are the most significant element in oil companies' decisions both on stock levels and in the financing costs of capital-intensive oil production. They are also significant as either symptom or instrument of domestic monetary policy in oil consumer countries where interest rate levels affect both general economic activity and the real burden of the cost of oil on consumers.

If for prolonged periods real interest rates are negative, the value of money will tend to fall, real oil prices will fall and consumption will rise. Conversely, if real interest rates are high then money paid for oil supplies will maintain its value and there will be no propensity for consumers to respond to falling real prices by increasing physical demand.

The real supply and demand for oil, and hence fluctuations in the price of oil, seem to be governed principally by real US dollar interest rates. Even the potential for cartels to restrict production is more a function of consumer country monetary policy and historical declining US dollar value. US dollar interest rates are an excellent indicator of movements in the oil price for many reasons:

- Oil is a US dollar-priced commodity.
- The USA is one of the largest producers, consumers and traders in oil.
- US dollar interest rates are the best indicator of US inflationary pressures and hence the real cost of oil to American consumers.
- The US economy and currency are highly influential in industrial country economic activity.
- Real US dollar interest rates are the principal determinant of real world interest rates, of world inflation, of other currencies' dollar parities and therefore of other countries' real oil costs.
- Dollar interest rates are the most significant influence on oil stock costs and therefore on the propensity of oil companies and sovereign oil producers to hold stocks.
- Oil exporters receive dollar purchasing power and interest rates will affect the rate of conversion of dollars earned into their local currencies.
- As oil producers borrow dollars on the basis of their oil wealth, it is the servicing of real dollar interest costs which becomes a major influence on levels of production and there-

fore the world oil price.

Just as high real interest rates bring more stable industrial country demand patterns, so oil exporters are influenced by the same high interest rates to maintain production levels, indicating a lower and more stable oil price in both nominal and real terms. Any change in physical supply and demand will have immediate effects on the oil price which in turn will re-establish a balance of supply and demand. With lower inflation and a convergence of real and nominal oil prices, the transparency of market pricing increases and the adjustment of supply and demand will be so much quicker than during the 1970s so that oil prices should settle back to "pre-disturbance" levels. Indeed, given the relative speed of demand changes through fuel substitution and efficiency of use, compared with the long lead times from oil exploration to production, it is probable that "post-disturbance" price levels could well be lower than the previous "equilibrium" level.

Table 1 traces real dollar interest rates and their relation to changes in the official oil prices over the period 1965 to 1982. The period can be divided into five significant sections: 1965-69, 1970-74, 1975, 1976-80 and 1981-82. In order to compare the 1970-74 period when nominal interest rates were low and the 1976-80 period when nominal rates were very high, Table 1 shows real interest rates as a percentage of nominal rates. For all periods except the depths of the 1974-76 recession the real interest rate stimulus to oil price rises is significant when this measure falls below about 20 per cent.

We can see that the period 1965-69 was one of high real dollar interest rates and real rates were on average 33.4 per cent of nominal rates. This produced a stable official oil price for the period of $1.80. The 1970-74 period showed average negative real dollar interest rates and real rates were on average only −0.6 per cent of nominal rates. This produced an average annual oil price rise of 62 per cent over the period. 1975 can be regarded as the trough of the recession with very low real interest rates qualifying not as a stimulus to demand but rather as a reflection of low activity.

When US and OECD growth rates picked up again between 1976 and 1979 there was no return to the tighter monetary conditions of the mid 1960's when real interest rates as a percentage of nominal were over 35%. Instead real Dollar interest rates remained low or negative (see table 2) and thus stimulated further inflationary demand for oil between 1979 and 1981 after which recession and low growth returned between 1981 and 1983.

But this time the Governments in the USA, Britain and Germany led the way towards tighter monetary control and higher real interest rates and between 1981 and 1984 real Dollar interest rates as a percentage of nominal averaged 58% – a situation not experienced since 1965. Thereafter, whether in recession (1981-1983) or growth periods (1983-85) the oil price fell back. The fall was not as great as market conditions might have indicated because OPEC cut its own production by about 15m barrels per day from its peak in the early 1970's.

The continuation of high real interest rates in 1985 (and the resulting fall in inflation) has prolonged the falling oil price trend and a further decline in even the nominal oil price over the next few years is probable since the years 1981 to 1985 have seen the highest real interest rates since 1965.

Taking consecutive two year periods and comparing real interest as a percentage of nominal with the average oil price in the following two year period, a reasonable correlation emerges. (See Table 2). The period 1973-1976 does not yield a similar correlation as recession kept oil demand low and OPEC caution following a sharp drop in demand for its oil in 1975 prevented an early return to aggressive pricing.

Comparisons of such short periods are however of less value than the long term changes in monetary control and hence price stability. Taking four consecutive four year periods since 1965 we can demonstrate a strong causal connection between the monetary irresponsibility of Government and the subsequently inflationary effect on oil prices (see Table 3).

Inflationary pressure, brought about by Government's monetary policies is the principle cause of violent fluctuations in the price of all commodities. *Nominal* price changes distort the vital signalling function of real prices so that neither producers nor consumers can judge the true state of supply, demand or value of a commodity.

The fluctuation in the oil price has demonstrated the de-stabilising effect of political money printing very effectively. For some time the political disguise is effective and the recipients and savers of money are unaware of its decreasing real value. When they eventually start to test the market price the price rises dramatically. In the case of oil a cartel was able to take the price well beyond its true real value – (until sufficient oil production was then stimulated outside the cartel!) Firstly

23

recession (1974-76) and then the re-establishment of sound money (1981-1985) checked the ability of OPEC to impose rising prices.

Inflation is a deceit practised by Governments on its own people and those with whom it trades. The inefficiencies and political   privileges it is designed to conceal are eventually revealed and those who have benefited from artificial prices and artificial power (whether Trade Unions and Industry at home or commodity producers abroad) are forced to produce genuine value. They then receive real market prices from responsible consumers, not the inflated currency of corrupt Governments.

Table 1: Oil prices, real interest rates and economic growth

YEAR	1965	66	67	68	69	70	71	72	73	74	75	76	77	78	79	80	81	82	83	84
annual rise in official oil price %	–	–	–	–	–	–	24	12	40	235	–2	7	9	–	46	66	10	–11	–9	–
real US dollar interest rate	2.2	1.9	1.5	1.1	1.2	.5	–	.8	.8	–3.2	–3.3	–.8	–1.2	1.15	.8	1.4	7.28	8.6	6.4	6.5
real interest as % of nominal	55	39	35	20	18	7.8	–	19	11	–41	–56	–16	–22	13	6	10	43	65	66	60
OECD real growth	5.2	5.3	3.7	5.8	5.4	3.6	3.8	5.3	6.1	.9	–.4	5.9	3.7	3.8	3.4	1.3	1.2	–.5	2.7	4.0

Sources: International Financial Statistics, OECD, National Westminster Bank.

Table 2

Real as 0% of nominal Dollar interest rates		average annual oil price rise/fall	
1967-68	28%	1969-70	0%
1969-70	13%	1971-72	18%
1971-72	4%	1973-74	130%
1977-78	−4.5%	1979-80	66%
1981-82	54%	1983-84	−5%
1983-84	63%	1985-86	−10%

Table 3: Real interest rates and prices

YEAR	1965-69	1970-74	1976-80	1981-84
real as a percentage of nominal rates	33.4%	−0.6%	−1.8%	55%
average annual oil price rise	0%	62%	24%	−2.5%

4   A Myth About Inflation

Introductory Note:
For nearly two years the author wrote a monthly column in a business magazine. Entitled "Economic Myths" it aimed to question and analyse some of the more common cliches used in the debate on political economy. One particular "myth" excited much comment, in reply to which the following letter was published.

The recent "Myth", "A lower pound means higher inflation", excited some criticism. This is not surprising since this particular myth is by far the most widespread and pernicious in the political and economic debate.

There are two basic issues – the definition of inflation itself and the connection between inflation and the fall in the exchange rate.

The rise and fall of an exchange rate is like the rise and fall of the price of any commodity. It acts as a signal of the changing balance of supply and demand for the currency or commodity. Such adjustments occur whether there is inflation or not. However money and its price is crucially different from other commodities because it is also the medium of exchange for other commodities. We price other commodities in terms of this particular commodity. Inflation is not a function of the change in prices of various commodities, it is solely a function of the decline in the value of money itself. Such changes may affect the exchange rate but the change in the exchange rate cannot in itself affect the rate of inflation.

Inflation is always a function of the supply of money increasing out of all proportion to the rise in the supply of goods and services which people are prepared to buy. Unfortunately the word inflation has come to mean, in common parlance, "a rise in the Retail Price Index". But the RPI does not measure the decline in the value of money (ie inflation) it measures the rise and fall of some prices, prices which would be rising and falling for very healthy reasons even in the absence of inflation. Indeed the RPI is so perverse as to measure as "inflationary" a rise in interest rates which will contribute to a reduction in the supply of money and hence to a fall in prices! The fall in the value of the pound may of course have many and varying causes. An oil bouyant economy like the UK's will suffer a fall in its currency if the oil price falls. We may import more than we export. Foreign companies may be remitting heavy dividend payments abroad. We may be investing more abroad than foreigners are in the UK. All these are real economic causes of a lower exchange rate. The fall will readjust international comparative prices and we *may* then export more, import less, make less outward investments and see the pound's level rise again. Or we may not be able or willing to do these things, so the pound stays low. The pound has declined against all major currencies for many decades, even when inflation was not an issue, merely because we no longer enjoy a dominant, imperial position in the world. Our currency declined in the non inflationary 1950's and rose strongly in the inflationary 1970's.

However there is a further cause of a falling pound – the fact that we create too many pounds and their value falls externally just as it does internally. This is an inflationary fall not because it causes inflation but *because it is a result* of inflation. However as we see from the late 1970's example, domestic money creation led to a falling pound up to 1976 but this was unable to counterbalance the positive factor of having discovered 25 years of oil reserves under the North Sea and having started to produce and export oil.

One of my critics maintained that a fall in the value of the pound did reduce demand in the UK (assuming of course that we continued to import at the same rate) but that this would be offset by increased exports. This *may* happen in the *long* term but the immediate impact is of lower demand (not higher inflation!) picking up in increased exports much later (the "J curve" effect). However as we have observed of the UK economy the increase in import prices has resulted in our repeatedly slipping down the first part of the "J" and never rising again! Governments counter-acted the fall in demand by printing money to accomodate the new higher price of imports. Had they done nothing the increased prices of imported commodities would have been balanced by a fall in domestic goods prices – ie not inflationary. However their inflationary route temporarily sustained import levels and resources were switched neither to import saving nor to export promotion. But the point is that even if this process of a falling exchange rate (and no Government inspired inflation) led to more domestic demand from export sales to compensate for higher import prices, the lower pound would still not have raised prices in general and so would not have been inflationary.

28

The inflationary Government *response* to structural economic failure *caused* a fall in the pound. The erroneous assumption that the reverse was the case excused further Government inspired inflation. In reality either of the two *real* explanations would have meant radical changes in the structure of industry and/or a radical change in Government monetary policy – both far less politically palatable than playing the inflation game – and blaming the exchange rate!

Although I wrote in the inflation Myth ". . . a mere fall in the external value of the pound is not in itself *inflationary* – indeed it is *deflationary"* I did not intend to suggest that these were opposite terms. On the contrary I meant to point out that the two expressions concerned completely different issues. Inflation concerns *money* demand – and it's excess. Deflation concerns *real* demand – and its lack. Lack of demand caused by higher real prices will be adjusted by a re-allocation of resources but an excess of money demand created by Government inspired inflation can only be cured by Government.

Individuals and corporations only act rationally if confronted by rational signals. If those signals are distorted by inflation or aggregated out of all connection with reality by economists, they are worthless and economic activity grinds to a halt. I have tried to focus attention on *real* movements in prices and exchange rate in an economy in which supply, demand (and economists' nomenclature) have not been distorted by the scourge of inflation. After 20 years of monetary decadence it is evidently as great a struggle for economists as it has been for businessmen!

5 Making Monetarism Work (1981)

"Excellent" Milton Friedman

MONETARIST SUCCESS – POLITICAL FAILURE

The Conservative Government set out to reduce public borrowing but the burden of debt has risen. It set out to reduce taxation but the burden of taxes is now greater. It set out to promote small businesses but they have been decimated. Most important of all – for this was the key to all reforms – it set out to make people responsible for their actions but has succeeded only in making the responsible bear the consequences of the actions of the irresponsible.

It is the failure of politicians to carry out actions for which they are uniquely qualified – political actions – which threatens economic disaster, for the underlying social and economic privileges and distortions of which inflation is merely a symptom can only be remedied by Government action.

The Conservative party was elected on a mandate to restore the health of the UK economy by decreasing the claims of the public sector on national resources, restoring and maintaining the value of money and where possible returning decision making to the market place where choices made are both more democratic and more efficient. Apart from strict macro-economic management, the main element of which is control of the monetary aggregates, there is implicit in a return to market decision-making an obligation to remove the gross imbalances of institutional and collective power. If left unchecked under the zero sum regime of monetarism then imbalances will lead to even more serious misallocation of resources than under Keynesian "inflationism".

THE LIMITED CONTRIBUTION OF MONETARISM

Before trying to determine the conditions under which "monetarism" will succeed we must understand why Keynesian demand management and deficit financing increasingly failed to perform in the way Keynes had intended. The gross distortions of power in our economic and social life have the same critical effects on both monetarist and Keynesian strategies. Although fiscal manipulation and control of money supply are both blunt aggregate macro economic tools the latter has one inherent advantage – that it *reveals* the location and extent of market distorting power and privilege for all to see.

When Keynes was writing his thesis and during the post war years when western governments to a greater or lesser extent indulged in Keynesian demand management, the institutions which today so radically distort both the economic and political markets had not established themselves following the social upheavals of the Second World War. For some time counter cyclical deficit financing, coupled with the political strength to prime demand through capital projects rather than current expenditure, fed through relatively undistorted capital and labour markets to re-establish equilibrium at higher levels of activity and employment. Gradually, however, demand stimuli served only to ensconce the market-distorting power of political interest groups, nationalised industries and monopoly labour and hence increased the frequency and extreme fluctuations of business cycles. It was to reverse this trend that Mrs Thatcher's government chose monetarist constraint which reveals economic distortions and the social market economy to re-establish balanced growth. The fact that there has been a failure to control money supply has not paradoxically mitigated the disastrous effects of real power imbalances in our economy because a high sterling exchange rate and high (but not high enough!) interest rates have been as revealing as real control of money supply would have been.

MONETARISM AND IRRESPONSIBLE BEHAVIOUR

The Labour government's incomes policy did not bring down inflation: it kept unemployment down by curbing the power of certain monopoly suppliers of labour goods and services. This government has decided rightly that incomes policies distort relative prices and hence economic efficiency. However, in the absence of both an incomes policy and radical reform of the labour market, the only result is that any group in the non-market sector which achieves an excessive pay rise does so at an

31

exact and equivalent cost to other workers. Inflationist money-printing governments would, of course, have transferred resources away from that powerful group of workers by devaluing money balances and paying all wage earners more. This option is not open to this government. The chances of reducing inflation and increasing employment rest on the effectiveness of monetary control and the removal of the power and privilege enjoyed by government, groups of workers and corporations and vested in them by statute, tradition and indifference.

The tools of monetary control are inadequate and must be strengthened. However, in the light of the gross exploitation by trade unions in the non-market sector of those less privileged it is perhaps as well that monetary policy has failed. Success in limiting the growth of money supply would have forced the market sector to pay for the privileges of others with far higher unemployment than we have today. To infer from our present troubles – as even many Conservatives do – that monetarism has failed is a travesty of the truth. The practitioners of monetarism have failed in their technical control and politicians have failed to reform the obscene imbalances of social and economic power. The expectation of "moderation" in pay claims in the present round seems to have been based *entirely* on the assumption that high and rising unemployment would deter trade unions from unrealistic wage settlements.

The assumption that as monetary constraint reduces inflation then expectations of future price rises will fall and wage claims moderate has little to commend it. If past wage rounds had exhibited such rational behaviour, average wages would not have risen by 25% in 1974-75 when prices had never previously risen by more than 12%. Equally, when year on year inflation dropped to 8% during 1977-78 why did the following year see wage rises of over 15%? If we (rightly) see no Philips curve trade off between rising inflation and lower unemployment we must never rely on the assumption that rising unemployment will bring about lower inflation. However, in the absence of radical reform of monopoly public services that is precisely what we shall be relying on. Just as the money illusion on which inflationists have relied soon wears off and rising inflation eventually leads to fewer and fewer jobs, so unemployment, almost regardless of its level, ceases in the end to frighten wage bargainers unless the number of unemployed keeps rising. The vicious circle of intimidation finally ends in social disintegration. The government cannot, having embarked on a strict monetary policy, rely on temporarily reasonable consensus decisions from powerful market defying groups. If we were relying on this then we may as well have an incomes policy! If we are not prepared to act against the irresponsibility of collective and institutional power then an incomes policy is our only course.

THE PUBLIC SECTOR – RULES FOR RESPONSIBILITY

The public non traded sector includes all those areas in which goods or services are not traded (e.g. fire service, army, police, inland revenue). Here the sole criterion for pay determination should be the need to recruit or retain suitable staff. An application to raise the remuneration for certain jobs or grades must show statistical proof of lack of applicants of a suitable standard. If jobs outside these sectors in the market sector are more attractive then this will be demonstrated by the market and the price paid for particular employees must therefore rise. Attempts to find justification for pay rises unrelated to supply and demand for labour have led to both shortages and over-supply in the same industries. There can be no question of "signing agreements" with groups of workers like doctors, firemen or policemen guaranteeing them a job or a certain wage level linked to other workers – unless, of course, the government would care to underwrite such privileges for all market sector workers. Perhaps we can guarantee that BL cars will always be sold at a price to give shareholders the same return as Ford shareholders? Or that shopkeepers will always sell their goods at margins which will give them a standard of living equivalent to a civil servant? The relating of non market sector remuneration to those working in the market sector provides the only true "comparability" and is superior to both cash limits and incomes policies. As far as the public sector is concerned the only difference between an incomes policy and cash limits is that under the latter, unions merely decide how many of their colleagues need to be dismissed to provide the cash for what the unions *believe* is a just settlement! The power of such groups must be removed, for when an economic upturn starts the old bottlenecks will persist and public sector unions will force even this government to fund their privileges by pricing the market sector out of capital investment. The basic method of controlling the abuses of the public non-market sector adopted by the government is cash limits which in theory allow the trade unions and public sector to bargain for more than the rise in the cash limit provided that any excess is paid for by sacrifices elsewhere. However, either unions bargain away the jobs of their colleagues or the public sector employer cuts the services provided. Cash limits are therefore infinitely less attractive than an incomes policy in the non-market sector, although both suffer from being politically determined. When government uses arbitrary political judgement to determine rewards then they are morally and logically open to the pressures of institutions imposing *their* political determination of economic rewards.

The market public sector (e.g. British Steel, National Coal Board) does however compete with other suppliers at home and abroad. Apart from setting a target return on assets and preventing abuse of market dominating positions, the government should not intervene to determine pay, and wage bargaining will reflect the profitability of the business, provided that there is national and international competition for the provision of goods and services and that government does not intervene to subsidise and protect. The presence of the closed shop and other *politically* unpalatable phenomena does not ensure irresponsibility or privilege, rather it is the context within which trade union bargaining is conducted. Responsibility is learned through experiencing the constraints of the commercial world. The correlation between the closed shop and high wage settlements is not high, while there is a very high correlation between high wage settlements and protected or monopoly industries. If the exploitive power of protected bargainers is not curtailed by exposure to commercial constraints there are only two solutions – either a proliferation of such arrangements as less organised labour (white collar, professional) seek to re-establish differentials by taking themselves "out of the market" or the advent of a genuine socialist state – welcomed by the middle classes! – which would abolish collective bargaining altogether.

In those public sector industries (Post Office, British Gas, British Rail) where a "natural monopoly" exists, the "profits" which accrue are the result of monopoly pricing and therefore cannot be the subject of wage bargaining. Collective bargaining can only be permitted if it takes place between employers and employees who are responsible to the market – i.e. where the consumers of a product or service are capable of taking their custom elsewhere. There are, of course, various ways in which an element at least of market constraint can be brought to bear

34

on the natural monopolies: Auctioning franchises to the private sector for parts of public networks or imposing prices for public services which are automatically linked to market commodities or opening up e.g. gas, rail and electricity networks as "common carriers" for the private sector. Not only would such market involvement permit collective bargaining but there would then exist a commercial framework within which the utilities concerned could make national *responsible* decisions about the cost of and return on capital, thus permitting free access to the capital markets. The pricing record of the nationalised industries under this Conservative government is an utter disgrace for a party which must regard monopoly pricing as immoral in any climate never mind at a time of recession. When the intention had always been to denationalise, demonopolise and restructure the public sector to legtimise *existing* prices, it was a particularly hypocritical move to allow nationalised industries to *raise* their monopoly prices by 30% in one year. To transfer public sector borrowing via nationalised industry price rises to private sector borrowing is totally irrelevant to the growth in bank lending and money supply. The only result is the accommodation of public sector failure and a ruthless squeeze on British industry.

WHICH PSBR?

The Government's attitude towards nationalised pricing betrays an apparent misunderstanding about the relationships in the public and private sectors. PSBR is as relevant to monetary control where the "P" stands for "private" as where the "P" stands for "public". Whether the borrowing requirement be public or private the only question of importance is how will it be financed, through the banking system (inflationary) or from the sale of bonds to the non-bank private sector – the ability of both government and industry to do the latter depends on the level of inflation and inflationary expectations. Ironically it has been the very tools of monetary control which have produced the politically most damaging institutional distortions. The clearing bank cartel has garnered rich reward from their low cost of funds and high interest rates, distributing unparalleled largesse to their employees and becoming (by net income and net worth) the richest banks in the world. The cumulative profit of the clearing banks must have further contributed to the expansion of bank lending and hence money supply. The pursuit of a tight monetary policy requires either a windfall profits tax or a call for supplementary special deposits from clearing banks to siphon off profits which high interest rates alone have bestowed. The 1981 windfall profits tax may have to be repeated since bank taxation (thanks to leasing and withholding tax loans) has not reflected bank profitability.

As British industry has failed to receive or react to commercial stimuli to invest, successive governments have turned to sundry fiscal allowances in order to tempt resources towards those areas politicians thought worthy of investment. The maze of tax allowances – stock relief, small business subsidies and relief, subsidised interest rates, tax relief on small business investment, bank loan guarantees etc. had become necessary to counteract the investor's historical experience of negative returns and of course the effect of the government's own tax incentives to invest in house purchase, pension and life insurance. The pathetic waste of public money on mutually conflicting tax allowances must end so that funds can once again flow through an undistorted market and seek a real rate of return.

THE SMALLER COMPANY SQUEEZED

Whilst the clearing banks reap their harvest, British industry is by no means universally squeezed, for here too the disparity of industrial power, inflation, and past governments' intervention have combined to decimate the smaller enterprises. Whereas the large companies could squeeze their smaller suppliers by delaying payment and borrow excessively on overdraft to play the stock relief game and round trip in the money markets, smaller enterprises could not control their debtors, could not compete in a stagnant market with wages paid to monopoly labour in larger firms, and could not offset interest costs against taxable profits since they weren't making any. Just as the small company can be forced to finance the large company in recession so the manufacturer who supplies a monopsonist retailer can be forced to sign agreements which transfer the burden of a recession away from the retailer to the manufacturer. Small firms dependent on large concerns as buyers and/or suppliers are squeezed in a recession as the large firm is in a position to cut credit terms to purchasers and lengthen the period before payment to suppliers. Some form of fiscal control could penalise those companies who, in a recession, are seen to benefit unduly from this process.

LOCAL AUTHORITY'S ACCOUNTABILITY?

Another area of public non market activity – the local authority – is deemed to be responsible to a market – the political market. However, since the most profligate authorities enjoy the support of those who are never in danger of paying for the policies for which they vote and those who foot the bill often have no vote at all, it is evident that there exists here *no* kind of market. Central government must therefore continue to intervene until there is a sufficient reform of local authority funding to permit direct economic responsibility of the electorate for political decisions taken on their behalf.

Mr Heseltine's anguish, shared by rate-payers, will only be multiplied by present policies. Reasonable local authority behaviour is a function of direct responsibility for their actions. As with nationalised industries the structural reforms must come first, not the undiscriminating sledge-hammer of grant withdrawal.

SUMMARY

Monetary control is incompatible with fiscal indiscipline. Public spending beyond the means of the public purse, on activities unrelated to market demand is both a cause of high inflation and unemployment and more significantly a symptom of gross distortions of supply and demand for goods and services brought about by the power and privilege of certain groups.

The electorate is programmed to anticipate a reversal or softening of the Government's approach. Borrowers and house speculators are poised to take advantage of negative interest rates as the government devalues the money balances of the weak to pay for the privileges of the strong. As votes become more important than honesty, the electorate expects the government to turn a blind eye to wage rises and to subsidise incompetence. And what is to stop the repetition of historical mistakes by Mrs Thatcher? Have collectivist power and non market privilege been neutralised? Have monopolies of capital and labour been dispensed? Is society now transparently more just than before May 1979? The answers to these questions must – sadly – be "No". Politicians, not monetarists, have failed. We must all accept the responsibility for our own actions. This government's failure has been not in its economic convictions but in its political failure to act.

6   The Moral Basis of Monetarism (1984)

"I found it fascinating" Milton Friedman

"I read it with pleasure and a very large degree of agreement" Mancur Olson

"Very good indeed, I commend it strongly"
Rt Hon David Howell

Many Western Governments, having embarked on a monetarist policy as a principal ingredient in their economic programmes were inevitably going to be confronted with a stark choice. Monetary control would be a shorter, more immediate and less overtly political process than the rationalisation of their 'real' economies. The real 'crunch' would occur if the effects of monetary control, combined with electoral pressures, conflicted with the slow implementation of political reform. At such a point Governments would have to choose either to adhere to monetarism, confident that their radical "marketisation" and removal of Government and institutional distortions would quickly increase the efficiency of 'supply' or to abandon monetarism and 'stimulate demand' in order to prevent those distortions from further punishing the innocent with mass unemployment.

The latter recourse to the disastrous policies of the past may yet be forced upon governments by their own failure to tackle the underlying *political* causes of western economic decline which the practice of monetarist responsibility has so well revealed. The excessive pre-occupation on both sides of the Atlantic with the technical measurement of money and the 'defeat of inflation' was never as important as the social analysis of *why* Governments found themselves in the position of "printing money" and promoting inflation.

In Britain there are those who arrived at the monetarist practice, not principally through intellectual insight but through moral outrage at the long process of economic decline, social decadence and political opportunism which had characterised British life for 25 years or more. For them the printing of money was the ultimate immorality and the final symptom of government accommodation of the powerful and privileged. The morality of monetarism is in its analysis of this complete reversal of the traditional role of Government.

Monetarism and the morality of the market place do not reduce the power of the state – they strengthen it in its true role as the arbiter of fair play, the controller of the strong, the protector of the weak. That is the morality which was lost as the post war generation used the state to intervene to protect their established privileges, shore up their decaying industries, promote union and professional power and preserve political sinecures. The cost to other was disguised by inflation. The *economic* control of money has put an end to this method of disguise and revealed a far more complex *political* message. Monetarism is the first vital and indispensable step towards the revelation of economic inefficiency and political opportunism in British society. There must be no guilt ridden timidity about the role of monetarist policy in the mistaken belief that the revelation of long concealed problems is the cause of those problems. Monetarism is the morality which prevents the devastation of the savings of the old, the surreptitious accommodation of undemocratic power and the lies and deceit of government. It is and must remain a moral crusade. No monetarist analysis of the present can be anything but an angry condemnation of the past. This paper attempts to analyse the root causes of the maldistribution of power in society, the political nature of the causes of economic decline, their revelation through monetarist practice and the radical political steps which must be taken to promote economic and political democracy. The analysis can to a great extent be applied to all the economies of the western industrialised democracies. There is no solution to domestic economic problems without stability in the international economy but the latter depends totally on the political will to restructure the domestic economies of democratic nations.

Definitions

It is all too easy in the heat of political debate to use words and concepts which are not received by the reader as they were understood by the writer. The following is an attempt to minimise such potential misunderstandings.

MONETARISM

A monetarist assumes that changes in the supply of money and credit in the economy is the prime casual factor in long run changes in the general level of prices. Monetarism is the *financial* analysis of the symptoms resulting from government action. However significant such an analysis is, it is of infinitely less importance than the *economic* analysis of the use or waste of real resources and the political motivations of government in the inflationary process.

THE WRONG CONSENSUS

The Wrong Consensus is government based on the accommodation, (disguised by the process of inflation), of the demands only of those powerful enough to threaten the Rule of Parliament. Since this accommodation is based on the defiance of the politically and economically expressed wishes of their fellow citizens the Wrong Consensus is diametrically opposed to the genuine democratic consensus.

ILLEGITIMATE POWER

Illegitimate power is power which once acquired through the machinations of the Wrong Consensus is not open to challenge either through Parliament or the market place. Outside the many legitmate roles of the State, Government promotes the retention of illegitimate power by preserving institutions which the people acting in free association would have condemned to oblivion. Within the Rule of Law only the market mechanism can balance the relative claims of those who possess and those who must have the right to challenge that possession.

PRIVILEGE

Privilege is the arbitrary possession of illegitimate power. Since there will always be social variety and change, so there will always be relative degrees of wealth and power. The destabilisation of society comes not from variations in wealth and power but in the arbitrary and unchallengeable possession of any particular degree of wealth and power.

LEGITIMATE POWER

Legitimate Power is power which is open to social challenge. Economic power accruing through "money votes" is more direct, immediate and, in a competitive environment, less open to distortion than political power accruing through periodic electoral votes but the latter is the only potential check on the anti-competitive practices of the economically powerful.

THE POLITICAL MEANING OF MONETARISM

There is no reason to assume that monetarism belongs to any particular part of the political spectrum. It can be embraced with equal enthusiasm by left and right. Those who wish to destroy the status quo will oppose it, those who wish to maintain the economic and political system will adopt monetarism, for the practical effect of accepting the scientific analysis is to maintain confidence in the currency, the method of exchange of goods and even political ideas. Even the linguistic currency is upheld for in the *absence* of monetarist constraints, the government's debasement of the currency turns financial promises into lies and industrial agreements into deception. The debased language no longer has reliable meaning; the logical framework of our existence is destroyed, the morality of social relationships usurped. This applies to any status quo-communist, fascist or social democrat, Conservative, Labour or Liberal. Monetarism is politically neutral, as is inflation.

Typically those who find they can no longer afford something blame "inflation". Inflation itself however does not prevent people buying what they could previously afford since inflation in itself is merely the devaluation of money not the raising of relative prices (or lowering of relative wages). If 10% more money is "printed" then everyone's money will be worth that much less. Although therefore demand rises and hence prices by 10%, no one is poorer than before since in real terms no goods or services are more expensive than before. Where therefore the complainant can justifiably identify himself as poorer it is not inflation he should blame but *the deliberate transfer of wealth from himself to other partially disguised by government inspired inflation.* But how much more convenient for the beneficiaries and government that this transfer of wealth is not identified and the impersonal "deus ex machina" "inflation" is repeatedly blamed.

We must therefore seek the real economic and political causes of our decline not in the *symptoms* of inflation but in the *motivation* for inflation. By removing the monetary causes of inflation we are confronted not by a materialist and purely economic definition of our social ills, but we are increasingly conscious of the intensely *political* nature of the maldistribution of social power. Paradoxically the lessons of monetary analysis force government to return to purely political measures and away from the superficial tinkering with macro-economic levers, a pre-occupation in which post war Keynesianism had tragically persuaded them to indulge.

The correlation of world monetary growth and subsequent inflation since the second world war is impressive. The process of international liquidity creation through governments, and the banking system had remarkably simultaneous effects in all OECD countries, resulting in overstimulation of the house market, commodity and property speculation, a rise in precious metal prices and in the UK in 1973 to a near banking collapse.

It has been a common symptom of government money printing that individuals in London, Washington or Bonn could earn more from the appreciation in the value of their houses than from their annual salaries throughout the 1970's. Never was there a more cynical reflection of the relative value of labour and unproductive speculation. Today, as the governments in those capitals apply their stringent macro-economic policies to "bring down inflation" they succeed in doing so only by bringing economic activity to a halt and bankrupting market sector corporations. Either they do not recognise or they will not see their duty to reform the institutional distortions, privilege and corruption which underlie the *symptoms* of inflation and unemployment.

Now that the monetary squeeze in western economies has produced a politically unacceptable level of unemployment, governments have decided that a loosening of their monetary policy is preferable to electoral defeat. The third and only honest course of action, to tackle government inspired or tolerated waste of national resources, has been virtually ignored.

In the U.K. the government continues to encourage investment in housing and pensions rather than wealth creation and compounds the many corporate fiscal distortions by giving generous tax allowances to rich investors in small companies. The massive portion of national assets in the hands of nationalised industries continue to be used for negative returns. Even a market orientated government calls the (occasional) extracted *surplus* of public sector monopolies a "profit", prevents the import of coal to appease a monopoly trade union, and takes arbitrary non market decisions about the remuneration of policemen and nurses. Trade Unions still possess monopoly power to cajole their members and hold employers to ransom, not in the cause of a fair distribution of profit between capital and labour but in the pursuit of individual and collective political power. Hundreds of millions of pounds are still poured into loss making production of ships and steel while government spending as a share of GNP (even boosted by massive North Sea revenues) is higher than in 1979. While condemning Keynesian deficit financing of public investment government justifies a 20% rise in inflationary defence spending. While rejecting the superficial tinkering with *economic* symptoms a massive 20% rise in spending on law and order concentrates exclusively on *social* symptoms.

In the United States the government grants tax relief on interest for unlimited personal borrowing, authorises massive increases in the least market constrained and most inflationary areas of government spending – defence and space exploration, has re-allocated federal spending to states pretending that somehow that is more efficient, provides massive market distorting guarantees and subsidies for industry, and, like the U.K., provides tax incentives for investment in pensions and life insurance as if such investment without tax incentives would be ignored! There are 'Buy American' provisions to promote domestic industrial incompetence and although Trade Union membership is very small certain strategic areas like steel and transport are dominated by excessively powerful market distorting Unions.

In Germany the industrial sectors which provided the 1950's and 1960's "Wirtschaftswunder" are in relative decline as rapidly industrialising developing coutnries provide keen competition in Germany's export markets. Energy poor and lacking a firm base in services, computers and electronics, Germany nevertheless has acquired since the war a burden of State distributed largesse, an overburdened public sector infrastructure, comfortable industrial work practices, a vast wasteful health industry and large guaranteed (and unfunded) pensions for an increasingly ageing population.

In France, even before Mitterand's radical extension of State ownership and State distributed social largesse, industrial structure was geared to sectors where government purchases are dominant – armaments, nuclear, aerospace, railroads and telecommunications. Even the consumer oriented car manufacturing sector is heavily influenced by government ownership while the overall financial structure is dominated by government underwritten and manipulated commercial banks. The strong educational technical and career links between government, civil service and industry in this mercantilist State will have a deleterious effect on a centrally controlled inflexible system which will in future not be able to rely on a constant supply of a newly urbanised peasantry grateful for industrial employment. Within the EEC France cannot continue to count on the German and British fiscal purse to solve their agrarian social problems.

deleterious effect on a centrally controlled inflexible system which will in future not be able to rely on a constant supply of a newly urbanised peasantry grateful for industrial employment. Within the EEC France cannot continue to count on the German and British fiscal purse to solve their agrarian social problems.

The common characteristic which threatens these countries is not industrial change or economic decline but the political power of privileged institutions who, refusing to change and adapt, succeed in passing on the consequences of their failure to the rest of society, while compounding the wasteful use of valuable national resources in the hands of those politically powerful enough to force government to finance their incompetence.

GOVERNMENT AND THE WRONG CONSENSUS

Economic failure does not arise naturally. It has to constructed, and it is constructed by those who have acquired sufficient power to frustrate the natural course of events whereby the needs of individuals are met by others and assets acquired by individuals can only be retained if they are well used in the interests of others. In order to act against the interests of their fellow citizens, or retain assets which are repeatedly utilised for negative returns, individuals and corporations must enjoy the active connivance of government in this retention of power without responsibility. The central role of government in this process cannot be over emphasised.

The insidious nature of their involvement is exemplified in the government's own robbery of those who have invested their savings in what are laughingly called gilt-edged stock. £100 invested in government consols in 1950 would be worth a mere £2.50 in real terms in 1982 (1). And yet, did not the government always say that what is in the interests of the State must also be in the interests of the people who invest? Did one not learn that government risk is second to none? But of course the government does give guarantees – of jobs for dockers and miners, of index-linked pensions for civil servants and these guarantees hold good. Not of course for those who invested the fruits of a life times labour in government stock. Nor for the retired Captain of the Queen Mary whose pension between 1968 and 1982 rose by 32% while the cost of living rose 400% (2). The only thing a government guarantee can guarantee is that someone else will be paying for that guarantee.

And yet, despite this central role in economic decline and political opportunism and despite their confidence in their own ability to run society, governments are the first to identify the reasons for decline in international symptoms like "high commodity prices", "world recession", "collapse of interna-tional monetary system" as if these were causal events, unjustly visited upon innocent governments by some *deus ex machina.* In fact, far from the domestic economy being a victim of external events, it is one of the main constituents and instigators of economic decline. The U.K. has, more than most countries, failed to maintain a responsible and stable economy preferring to tolerate incompetence and the waste of national and international resources in the corrupt purchase of votes. Whereas honest companies and individuals responsible to consumers for their activities adjusted to changing circumstances, government flouted economic rules by protect-ing the incompetent and extending the aegis of political patron-age to maintaining institutions which the people acting as individuals would have condemnd to commercial oblivion. In the long run of course, there is even a limit to government borrowing, money printing and corruption, but in the long run politicians do not stay in power. In the medium term they can, however, buy many years of power and patronage at the expense of economic decline and individual misery since "the average", "the aggregate", "the collective" mind can be so easily misled. Collective "democratic" decisions taken by committees both fudge issues in the name of consensus and deflect any criticism from individuals who were responsible. Indeed, members of committees may all individually disagree with a conclusion or recommendation which they nevertheless collectively espouse as the lowest common denominator. No wonder that when a committee gave miners a 25% pay rise in 1974, followed some deceptive months later by an equal rise in coal prices, the link between decision and responsibility for consequences is made neither by timing nor by reference to

47

individuals. Equally what of the committee which recommended in 1972 that dockers should have jobs for life? What consequences of that shameful corruption were borne by those making that decision? And yet such procedures have been the staple diet of the United Kingdom since the second world war. Incompetence without responsibility disfigured the domestic economy and the persistent economic decay by small indetectable steps, ran parallel with an equally persistent decay in the body politic. For if the political establishment will not tackle incipient economic decline for fear of compromising its political power (by offending those whose accrual of privilege is the root cause of decline) then privilege, market distortion and economic failure are further compounded. The instigation of corruption and incompetence in any governed society is always political and the resolution of those ills is political. Between this beginning and end are mere economic symptoms.

The ensconcing of political power and privilege, the use of government commands and financial indiscipline to appease the powerful and disguise the extent of irresponsibility, the eventual imposition of economic control, the revelation of the location and extent of privilege lead inevitably to the painful political solution. This process is both national and international but just as the link between political decadence and economic decline can be disguised, just as the impersonal decisions of committees hide the link between responsibility and power, so the removal of practical responsibility to the nebulous and distant "international context" compromises our understanding and honesty.

Having failed to check the power of the privileged and seeing the resultant economic failure and social suffering, government resorts to even more superficial tinkering with symptoms. Having so effectively reduced the returns on investment, more national resources are artificially forced into the same wasteful channels. Having allowed the irresponsible to rob the youth of their jobs, "job creation schemes" are funded by relieving their parents of their savings. And yet, paradoxically, the greater the disaster created by the paternalist state, the more the people turn to that state and the politicians who always claim, partly through ignorance, partly because of a desire for self-aggrandisement, that they can indeed alter the course of events. If we consider the power and almost universal involvement of the state in macro-economic, industrial and social intervention, this is not an unreasonable assumption. However, it is the nature of the state's involvement and its historical expansion through a combination of collectivist design and individual weakness which has been so disastrous.

Some derive power from economic success which accrues to them as they attract "money votes" from those whose needs and desires they satisfy through the production of goods and services. Others derive power from the democratic votes of the people who see in their Parliamentary and legal systems a power to check or reconcile contradictions, exaggerations or inequalities which the pure pursuit of self interest may produce. A nation's defence, social security for the poorest, monopolies and mergers legislation, would all be examples of activities not readily or more efficiently pursued by individuals or corporations.

Both pivots of community life – the market place and parliamentary representation while relying on each other for their efficacy, have within themselves the seeds of their own destruction. While those who pursue their self interest through commercial activity must adapt their behaviour to conform with fiscal and social responsibilities imposed by government, so government must preserve the power of free individuals to pursue their responsible interests without fear of the totalitarian judgements of the state. Market freedom without constraint can lead to competition which is destructive of the very framework necessary for healthy commercial activity. On the other hand the hybris of the all powerful State, by not recognising the limits of its effectiveness can soon earn the contempt of those it set out to protect, and the praise of those it set out to control.

In the United Kingdom – and to a greater or lesser extent in all Western capitalist democracies – it has been both the growing power and the increasing impotence of the State which has upset the balance of power. For whereas there has been no lack of social security, higher taxes and daily intervention in prices and incomes there has also been a paradoxical impotence to check the power of state industries, trade unions, local authorities, government agencies and certain professional associations.

The State has more power and yet the Welfare State is weak. Taxes are high and yet the tax take is pathetically low. Massive investment incentives exist and yet industry is weak. The underlying cause of this combination of power to act but impotence to effect any change is in the failure to define the legitimate roles of government. While Parliament indulges in extensive and complex legislation to nationalise industries, provide subsidies, and protect unions and industry from the consequences of their own actions, some of the most elementary tasks of government are neglected – to guarantee an efficient and just legal process, to keep roads and sewers in working order, to protect the individual from the tyranny of collective vested interests – to enforce, without favour, fair trading practices and anti monopoly legislation or to protect those like artists or writers who become the exploited victims of technical and commercial innovation.

The few legitimate activities of the State are the more vital and urgent as social and economic change accelerates.

Monetarism, as Sir Keith Joseph's pamphlet had it "is not enough". Norman St. John Stevas is correct when he writes: (3)

> *"Isolated from its political, social and moral context (monetarism) is . . . misleading and dangerous . . . our monetary policy has to be set squarely in the wider setting of traditional social concerns and traced to its roots in moral values".*

But neither he nor the government's critics in other parties are justified in believing that their boundless sympathy and endless compassion have done anything other than *in practice* bring about an immoral decline. For so often this compassion consists of what is called consensus politics. The Consensus politician is forever seeking political arrangements with economic symptoms rather than tackling root causes, for to tackle causes would lose his consensus.

A more exact analysis of this consensus reveals an (understandable) bias towards agreement with the most powerful institutions in the land – the very groups who, through their ability to acquire and retain power and privilege, influence the "democratic" process, waste the nation's assets and yet receive continued accommodation from the public purse at the cost of the majority of responsible citizens. When the rules of monetary recititude prevent this accommodation of the powerful through the printing of money and hence the theft of the savings and earnings of the weak, then "consensus" politicians find themselves *overtly* in the position of having to choose between the powerful and privileged and the ordinary responsible individual citizen. This overt conflict is not conducive to easy answers and electoral popularity so the "arid monetarists" become the scapegoats.

The attempts by politicians in "consensus governments" to paper over cracks and postpone politically unpalatable decisions or to take positive steps to "create jobs", "boost the economy" and protect the weak have in fact led to the opposite of all these aims. The riots of unemployed youth in the streets of the U.K. occurred in a country where job creation schemes had flourished for many years. Company bankruptcies had reached record levels despite massive tax allowances and subsidies. In the land of the welfare state over half a million stood in queues for important operations and yet the attempt to raise taxes for social welfare is met by widespread tax evasion by all sections of society. A compassionate people will the end but no longer grant the means because their leaders have squandered resources in bribing the powerful and protecting the privileged in those institutions who are responsible to the people neither through Parliament nor through the market place. It is guaranteed tenure, indexed pensions, the loss making steel plants and outdated pits which have absorbed the resources denied to the social services. If the problem for the government is the overhead of social spending as GNP falls in recession, the cause of that recession was not social spending. The irresponsibility of central and local government and the political aspirations of certain trade union leaders are directly responsible for the denial of jobs and security to youth which, having no voice in the corrupt halls of collectivist power, take to the streets in frustration and justified anger.

The politics which led to the riots were indeed the politics of consensus – but a dishonest and opportunist consensus between the powerful and the government. The real consensus has always been for the state to check, balance and control elements which threaten to dictate terms to the rest of society, not to appease them. However, consensus also requires that government act against those who may prove a threat to the "stability" of political power. There is always the time honoured reply to those who demand firm action that such action would be "politically unacceptable" and that the "public could not support it". Here is the crux of the failure of both democratic and economic institutions, for whereas personal responsibility for their individual actions is daily accepted by "the public", the decisions of government are concerned with the actions, freedoms and constraints of groups, institutions and the nation itself. To project personal comprehension of individual freedoms and responsibilities into a broader, national context and draw conclusions about legal constraints on collective action is difficult and requires intellect, insight, integrity and purposeful action from politicians who are prepared to lead. So much of the post war has seen the rise and establishment of the opportunist, the political fixer whose constituency has been some powerful interest group – nationalised industries, trade unions, the business lobby, academe, the professional associations. Those who rioted in the streets were the young, betrayed by their parents establishment, the black, who arrived too late to be part of the post war distribution of power and privilege, and the unemployed, who paid the price exacted by their ex work mates, still enjoying the protection of political and trade union patronage.

Such dispossessed minorities, in a society whose rewards and opportunities are determined by the "wrong consensus" are unable to challenge freely through their own efforts, education and skill for society's job opportunities. Too many professions have unacceptable barriers to entry, too many union closed shops are capable of achieving job protection and reward maximisation for their increasingly privileged members at the direct cost of those minorities excluded from those opportunities. There is for the youth and unemployed of Britain no transparently fair system for allocating jobs and rewards. They see only arbitrarily acquired (and therefore illegitimate) power in the possession of less qualified and not very industrious members of a club with a closed membership – the employed.

Since respect for the Law presupposes a respect for the method of distributing political and economic power it is little wonder that the threat to the Rule of Law should have arisen when the dispossessed youth of Britain took so dramatically and suddenly to the streets. If those riots were the result of *desperation* the present simmering frustration of the unemployed, in a country where rewards for those still in work are rising fast, could lead to a far more dangerous upsurge in the one vital ingredient for genuine revolution – the *aspirations* of the arbitrarily dispossessed.

The role of the market place in balancing the relative claims of those who possess and those who have the right to challenge that possession is at the very heart of the acceptance of the Rule of Law in a democratic society. All employee associations must accept the determination of their wages as the result of market forces so that the unemployed can have genuine opportunities to challenge for all available jobs. The opening up of employment opportunities will mean a radically different role for Trade Unions in the market sector who could choose to stop protecting jobs and bargaining for wage rates in return for the regular bargaining for the distribution of the returns on capital. Job opportunities would rise and incremental rewards would come in the form of "dividend".

The more rapid economic and social change becomes the more the patterns of wealth and power on which the Rule of Law is based must be open to scrutiny and challenge. Whether Government restricts opportunities directly or merely tolerates the monopoly power of employees it is contributing to all the dangerous tensions which the recognition of illegitimate power bring to the surface.

GOVERNMENT PREVENTS CHANGE

The power which has accrued to groups and individuals is a product of their economic success in satisfying the needs of their fellow citizens or their political success in being elected by the people to take certain decisions on their behalf. In a healthy society neither of these processes will have been tarnished or corrupted by the beneficiaries of them. From this "status quo" it is necessary to move on. Rewards for some must diminish, rewards for others must increase. Some factories must close, certain regions will decline, certain industries must revolutionise their activities, trade unions must discard traditional practices, certain highly paid professions find that manual labourers are commanding similar rewards, local authorities are losing their rate paying populations and some craft unions find that society no longer requires their craft. In all these circumstances change is required and the acceptance of a new reality less advantageous to the participants. To the extent that those so affected have acquired their rewards by being responsible to the people then they will understand and accept the judgement of time and adapt to the new circumstances. Just as they had no reason to feel guilty when they enjoyed the wealth or power provided by their fellow citizens through the market place or through electoral votes so they will have no resentment or anger when change and a lower status or level of reward are thrust upon them.

However, many have enjoyed their wealth and power without reference to their fellow citizens. They have frustrated democracy, usurped the law and distorted the market in their pursuit of power. The local authority or trade union leaders saw a political justification for their activities beyond the representation and defence of their constituents – they saw a permanent right to their own positions as the recipients and distributors of political and economic largesse. The fact that those they represented and the nation in general would benefit from abandoning old jobs and old assets for new more rewarding opportunities were irrevelant. Politically Arthur Scargill cannot afford to see NUM members becoming fewer and richer. The promotion of his socialist ambitions require that many men should continue to breath the dust of obsolete loss making pits and the monopoly structure and trading conditions of the nationalised coal industry provide him with the power to achieve this.

Equally intransigent in the face of change are the corridors of government where the privileges of non market rewards and index-linked pensions is the source of one of the most obscene divisions in society, the medical and legal professions whose regulations rival some of the worst excesses of trade union restrictives practices and the power of some well established companies in industry and commerce who seem to find a ready ear among Ministers of the Crown when new legislation is required to prevent the embarrassment of competition.

Government therefore finds it is worthwhile to avoid offending the powerful and proceeds to a "consensus" based on their requirements. If local authorities spend more than their revenue, if more funds are needed to subsidise loss making pits, if redundant railway lines are preserved, if the horrendous cost of inflation proofing civil servants cannot be found then it is borrowed. This involves the sale of public sector debt, a procedure whereby the populace is led to believe that if they lend the government £100 today they will get £100 back in, say, five years time. However, this money is borrowed, not to invest in wealth creating modern assets, but rather to shore up old wasteful assets and to pay interest on existing borrowings. Since the State's appetite for money becomes greater than the willingness of the people to lend, the government, therefore resorts to borrowing from the Banking system. The Government through the Bank of England controls and regulates the

Banks' reserves which as the basis of lending activity determines the rate of growth of bank balance sheets and hence the supply of money and credit in the economy.

The process of expanding the balance sheets of the Banks has rightly been described as government "money printing", since, as the amount of money created rises out of proportion to the rise in goods and services available in the economy so the value of money will fall. All those who hold monetary assets, like for instance bank or building society deposits or government stock, will see the value of those holdings diminish.

Note that those who tend to hold such assets are the poorer and younger members of society who are saving money in order to invest in their first real asset – a house. Note also that the old tend to invest their life savings in government stock and in building society deposits. Government money printing has devastated the savings of such people. It is theft and all the more invidious because the victims are never aware of the crime and indeed continue to vote for the perbetrators of the crime. As Hayek has observed as a characteristic of governments: "Dispensing gratuities at the expense of somebody else *who cannot be readily identified* became the most attractive way of buying majority support". (4).

This process of corruption started with the power of those in government, trade unions and industry whose activities were not open to the checks and balances provided by the people through the market place of Parliament. They were in a position to resist change and maintain their rewards despite failing the nation. They forced a weak state to accept the position and finance their privileges by robbing the young, the poor and the old of their monetary assets. But what kind of assets predominate among the powerful, those who have built and preserved a power base from which to defend their social position? Here we find ownership of two vital attributes – non monetary assets and monetary liabilities. Typical among the assets are houses, including second homes used primarily as "investments", land, jewellery and paintings. While the ownership of such inflation-hedging assets is of value in itself, the really profitable occupation when weak governments are printing money is the ability to borrow other peoples monetary assets to finance your own ownership of non monetary assets. As the savings of the pensioner disappear to a fraction of the value of his labour when he earned that money so the burden of the debt on the borrower declines and a windfall capital gain arises. Meanwhile, the young couple saving to buy a house see their savings eroded and the cost of houses rising out of reach. But for those who own a house there is actually a further incentive to borrow money – tax relief on the interest payments. Not only does government devalue the burden of house owners debt and give tax relief on borrowing, there is no tax to pay on the capital gain on the house when sold. The present government has further exacerbated this situation by raising the level of mortgage interest relief. This has further promoted housing as a market in tax avoidance. There is even evidence to show that much money raised for house purchase or improvement is in fact spent directly on consumer goods!

For those who, unlike the pensioner investing his life savings, see government stock as an opportunist short term investment, the state even arranges for capital gains arising on the sale of government stock to be tax free (if held for more than 1 year). Not only is this an insult to the long term investor but the true cost of financing government debt is concealed. Not content with deceiving the old and robbing the poor, the government adds insult to injury by providing gilt edged stock (low coupon gilt) specifically designed to help the rich high tax payer to avoid high taxes (he is able to take his interest as a capital gain). It may also be noted that while the government is in the corrupt process of distributing such largesse, it denies to industry, who would use such funds responsibly, the ability to raise money in the same way.

As the government struggles to rectify the results of its own dishonesty, we see at every turn that those whose power is at the root of economic incompetence and political corruption nevertheless emerge as beneficiaries. This is a characteristic of all societies which have an excess of *political* decision making processes. The most extreme examples are all socialist societies where the centralised control of political and economic life, through the Party and its committees is absolute and "democratic" collectivist decisions are taken about the definition and direction of aggregate phenomena. As societies advance from such primitive forms of control towards maximum individual freedom and responsibility the role of the state declines and decisions, political and economic are taken by emancipated individuals who are encouraged to plan, anticipate, act and accept the consequences of their actions. The State must now no longer "nanny" the weak but rather control the excesses of the strong, providing a rule of law and framework of standards and codes which all must obey. Within such a framework it is the disaggregated influence of individual decisions and preferences which bear upon all men. This is the nature of the market place. The less non-market so-called "democratic" decisions infringe upon society, the less opportunity exists for corruption by the powerful, firstly because the nature of market competition and change prevents the aggregation of power and secondly because the scope for circumventing the wishes of the people by *politically* powerful interest groups is reduced. There is therefore an inextricable connection in a democracy between monetarism, which reveals the extent and location of irresponsible power and privilege and the market philosophy which aims to dissipate such power and remove such privilege.

We have identified the following steps in the process of economic decline and political immorality.

1. Economic, political and social change begin to affect adversely the financial status of institutions.
2. Those who have acquired power without reference to their fellow citizens resist their loss of reward and status.
3. Government, because its power relies on at least the acquiesence of *politically* powerful groups, accommodates their wishes while maintaining the appearance of "moderate consensus".
4. The process of accommodating privilege and incompetence requires that government spends money it hasn't got by borrowing money which does not exist – hence inflation.
5. The jobs and monetary assets of citizens least able to defend themselves are taken from them by government in order to appease those who have been very successful in defending their privileges.
6. Money is devalued, as are promises, contracts and laws. Outmoded practices, decaying business, decadent institutions and wasting physical assets are preserved and the process of economic decline quickens.

What, then, if the monetary side of this process is halted? What are the effects of a refusal to print money?

THE IMPLICATIONS OF HONEST MONEY

There are of course any number of points along the spiral of decline at which a responsible government could begin the process of regeneration and most of them have been attempted over recent years: antimonopoly and restrictive practices legislation, control of nationalised industries, reduction in government borrowing and expenditure, trade union legislation and attempts to increase the accountability of central and local government. These steps have however largely failed because, without the understanding and support of electorate and elected, action against the irresponsible was politically impossible. The necessary insight and public support was not available *because the extent and location of irresponsible power and privilege was not transparent.* The process of decay and the accommodation of failure had built up an impenetrable web of economic and political obfuscation. The mere insight of wise officials and a brave government cannot, in a democracy, be sufficient to bring about reform. The process of change can only begin through a *general* insight into economic and political cause and effect which in turn can only be brought about by monetary constraint.

By limiting the growth in money supply to correspond more exactly to the real growth in the value of goods and services in the economy government deprived itself of the opportunity to print money. Although the *mechanics* of money creation allow it to be seen as passive – and hence money control as proactive – in reality the decimation of the people's savings (money creation) is active and the refusal to do so (monetary control) is passive. The pursuit of monetarism therefore is choosing *not* to continue with an immoral course. The government refused to "spend money it didn't have by borrowing money which didn't exist". When those powerful and irresponsible groups required a 'consensus' to be built around *their* demands at the disguised cost of other people's savings the government refused to accommodate them. Money demanded and taken by the strong is now an overt loss of competitiveness and therefore a threat to jobs (in the private market sector) and evident exploitation of consumers in the public non market sector. It becomes equally obvious that a rise in the price of public sector demands – (coal, electricity, rates, national insurance charges) has a direct effect on employment in the market sector. Private companies cannot, like the privileged public sector, pass on higher costs in a competitive market and must therefore resort to cost cutting, including redundancies.

The transparency of unjust cause and effect is of little short term comfort to the dispossessed. It is however of inestimable value to society in its attempt to establish a social order in which power cannot be retained by a minority at the cost of the majority.

When the theory of democratic representation was conceived, there was a justifiable belief that representation of all the people would provide both the means and the will to act decisively and without delay to rectify imbalances. It continues to be naively assumed that the first step towards rectification – i.e. the recognition of justice – is automatic. As we have seen the most obscene forms of injustice and exploitation are perpetrated surreptitiously so that the process of recognition followed by (genuine) consensus and then political action does not even begin.

The decision to control money supply and the concomitant refusal to accommodate economic failure reveals the location and extent of privilege *but in itself does not rectify the power imbalances.* Matching the growth in money supply to the growth in goods and services restores the meaning of promises, the honesty of contracts and the value of money but the equal revelation of the truth of economic and political relationships is unwelcome to politicians whose immediate response is vital. The final link in the process of reform (economic constraint, democratic recognition and *political* action) is missing. It is at this point that government is tempted to allow budget deficits and money supply to expand to "pull the economy out of recession" rather than to pursue their original intentions of rationalising the economy and allowing natural organic growth. This central point has now been reached in the U.K.

There was for too long an assumption by those responsible for Government economic policy that the re-establishment of honest money, the reduction in government spending and the "defeat of inflation" were sufficient to restore economic health. However, as we have seen the *real* causes of economic decline were not macro-economic but the political failure to check the power of institutions to frustrate change. Left unchecked under a regime of strict monetary control these power imbalances bring about an even more acute exploitation of the weak than under Keynesian "inflationism".

Recognising, as market economists do, the vital role of the

arbiter State, there must be doubts about the political course of the present government. Rather than act against the privileged there have been occasions on which the very same groups responsible for our present malaise have been accommodated while those who had acted responsibly have been crushed. Worst of all, instead of de-politicising the reward structure in the public sector, we have seen the political *(and therefore arbitrary)* distribution of largesse to groups like the Armed Services and Police according to no better criterion than that the present administration "thinks they deserve more pay". What happened to the principles of supply and demand here? Such principles have bankrupted good companies and reduced shopkeepers to poverty wages. What arbitrary right has the goverment to eschew market principles for its friends in the Police and Armed Services? Certainly, no more right than Arthur Scargill has to claim that miners should be paid as much as judges or that loss making mines should stay open. The depoliticising and marketising of the public sector is possible but like tackling so many of our social problems it requires the establishment of consistent principles and a strong political will. It requires more than a strong political will however when Goverment seeks to control what has been misleadingly called "public expenditure".

High (apparent!) taxation, large public sector borrowing and spending are rightly regretted but the mere reversal of these phenomena are as inadequate and superficial as the "defeat of inflation". Merely to reduce public sector borrowing will not necessarily contribute to the control of money supply or inflation (especially as much of the *private* sector is being artificially preserved by Bank of England lifeboats and by conscience striken Banks desperately trying to prevent the taxation of their windfall profits!). Merely reducing public sector spending on the "large overhead" of the welfare state in order to distribute it to the public sector monopolies (and hence to their trade unions) or to corporations and individuals through lower taxes is not only unjust but is *per se* irrelevant to promoting economic efficiency. It was not the sick, the old, or the unemployed who caused our economic decline but the active and the employed who allocated to themselves the nations valuable assets – skills, education, land, capital – and proceeded to reduce their value year by year because they had no market responsibility for the use of those assets. Without the most radical attack on the privileges of the non market sector the re-distribution of more pound notes in the form of reducing welfare and lowering taxes will further exacerbate the difference between the strong and the weak and will continue to channel funds to the irresponsible and incompetent who still have the power to grasp and squander those resources.

Despite the mistakes and understandable reticence to tackle traditional and entrenched institutional power, the combination of monetary constraint and public support for the first really principled and determined Prime Minister since the war, have brought about remarkable changes. Many public sector employees have launched themselves as independent companies, many local authorities have put services out to private tender when even trade unions have formed consortia to bid for work. (5). Telecommunications, gas supply and public transport have been forced to compete with commercial concerns. There is a new attitude among management, workers and consumers. Universities and schools are at last adapting to the real needs of the market place and in order to attract students who take a sober and rational view of study and work. The needs of the customer are increasingly recognised as paramount and profit is no longer quite such a dirty word. The people now see where the real extent of irresponsible power lies, recognising the strident demands of public sector monopolies and trade unionists as direct exploitation of the rest of society. By supporting underpaid nurses *and* the government simultaneously the people of Britain condemned those who for too long have had the power to allocate to themselves excessive rewards at the cost of less exploitive workers.

The public recognition of cause and effect, actions and responsibility becomes greater every day. These are the incipient characteristics of an honourable and emancipated society.

An emancipated society recognises that for individuals, institutions, and government, the enjoyment of freedom entails the acceptance of responsibility for the consequences of the exercise of freedom. The *ability* to understand the consequences of actions is derived for individuals and society as a whole from the long process of learning while the acceptance of responsibility for those consequences is a measure of moral maturity. As a society we learn by standing on the shoulders of past generations and as individuals we learn from our own observations and experiences of cause and effect. If political leaders anaethetise us from this learning process and forget or deny the lessons of the past, society is forced to repeat the painful learning process. If the true reflection of social relationships, cause and effect, success and failure and the process of change itself is disguised and distorted then there is no social recognition and no reponse. If the consequences of actions are dishonestly disguised then the individual does not learn, he becomes mindless, irresponsible *and increasingly dependent on the State which promotes the disguise.* A society of such individuals is helpless, frightened of itself and is forced to resort to further obfuscation, central control, a protective and oppressive State apparatus and further loss of freedoms for increasingly irresponsible citizens.

Emancipation is the political, economic and social release from this state of mindless dependence. The revelation of political privilege, economic distortions and commercial cause and effect are the unpleasant but necessary effects of strict monetarist policies. What was disguised is revealed. What was not understood is recognised. The people can now choose no path which is not clearly signposted. Social relationships are open to scrutiny. The market philosophy and the reduction of the State to its vital role as the controller of the strong, the protector of the weak and the dissipator of power open up new and endless possibilities for individual and institutional initiatives. Instead of drawing more and more people and resources into the political centre, where there is less and less insight, transparency or accountability, power is diffused to many diverse and responsive agents acting in commercial (and therefore democratic) response to the ever changing needs of their fellow citizens. Illegitimate power is recognised and eliminated. The more strident the privileged become in their condemnation of the revealers of that privilege, the more certain we are that change is upon us.

PRINCIPLES FOR GOVERNMENT ACTION

Trade Unions, conceived and promoted as market bargainers to seek a fair distribution of the returns on capital have become the controllers of markets and the extractors of wealth where it has not been created. They are, ironically, at their most exploitive where their socialist ideas have their fullest expression – in State owned monopolies!

Both the origins and justification for Trade Union bargaining are in the private market sector of the economy. When capital is used profitably, its owners benefit. It is accepted that the in the private market sector of the economy. When capital is used profitably, its owners benefit. It is accepted that the market value of workers will fluctuate and when labour is in surplus wages may not reflect a fair proportion of the joint product of capital and labour. It is therefore legitimate that free collective bargaining (undistorted either by a closed shop or a monopoly employer) should be concerned with the distribution of the returns on capital between workers and investors. Through such a system market returns for labour would be established in the private sector and those without jobs would be in at least as good a position as the employed to challenge for jobs, wages and returns on capital.

In the public sector, where Government has non market responsibilities decisions on costs and wage rates must be automatically market related. There can be no *wage* bargaining where the consumer is a captive of the (Government) producer. Pay determination must be through non Governmental "Standards Boards" which would not set pay levels but would monitor the standards of recruits and existing staff. If standards fell, Government would have to pay the market rate to "recruit and retain" employees of the right standard. Such a "depoliticisation" of public sector wage determination would remove *political* power from both Government and Unions, provide an automatic and transparent reward system and remove mutual suspicion between private and public sector employees.

Those who see a primarily "redistributive" role for taxation betray a misunderstanding of the power of capital in a competitive environment. Much of Trade Union legislation which enhanced the power of Labour in relation to Capital was an exaggerated and misguided response to the power of capital. That power arose not so much because Trade Unions were weak but because the strength of capital was not always open to challenge from the most powerful and egalitarian force in a free economy – competition. The combination of private capital, free consumers and competition means that neither the ownership of assets nor the income from them can ever represent "power" – and certainly in no *political* sense of the word power. Power to determine the use of these assets and size of returns on them resides instead with the consumer. Only in a socialist society is it possible to be permanently and unjustifiably rich. In a competitive capitalist society a rich man is continually called upon to justify his wealth by competitors and free consumers. This is the principal purpose of the privatisation of public assets. Attempts to use privatisation to raise maximum revenue (by restricting a competitive environment for the privatised concerns) would defeat the purpose of privatisation. Freedom for a pampered off-spring of the state would mean imprisonment for consumers and industrial suppliers.

Taxation therefore is largely irrelevant in the search for a "redistribution" of wealth. That is primarily the function of competition policy, for in a market environment decisions cannot be vulnerable to pressure group lobbying. Taxation on the other hand is entirely the prerogative of the Government machine, open as it is to the pressures of those who seek to achieve through Parliament what they have not earned in the market place.

The purpose of business is not to (a) raise revenue by (b) increasing production and (c) meeting demand. The purpose of business activity is to create value and hence wealth by providing new goods and services or increasing the utility of existing goods and services *in relation to their price*. This could in fact mean doing the opposite of a, b and c. It could mean cutting production of goods and services and revenue and ignoring the existence of demand for a product in order to introduce a completely new product – in smaller amounts with lower costs and price but of higher utility to the customer and hence of greater profitability to the producer.

All these healthy responses to perceived or anticipated *needs* rather than existing *demand* will be stimulated only if stable prices form a constraint on producers. If Government creates artificial money demand in the economy then the price of goods will rise to meet that new level of demand, producing an improved return to a producer *regardless of whether he has improved the quality, cost or pattern of supply*. Persistent Government subsidy through the "management" of *money* demand stultifies the reaction of businessmen to *real* demand and perpetuates outdated forms of supply.

The monetarist revolution has put a ceiling of price constraint on all markets so that the rewards for innovation and change from entrepreneurial suppliers are greater than for the traditional anachronistic "reactors" to Government manipulated and distorted demand.

Government is also constrained so long as monetary control is the paramount economic strategy. Whereas the constraint of price disciplines business suppliers, the constraint on money supply forces Government to pay for its excesses overtly and honestly either by raising interest rates or taxes, for both of which they will pay in votes.

This virtuous circle for business and political responsibility does unfortunately rely upon Governments being convinced of monetarist policies – unless of course we could enshrine such precepts in a written Constitution.

FOOT NOTES

(1) See "Equity and Fixed Interest Investment since 1919" de Zoete and Bevan January 1982 P.14-15.
(2) See Sunday Times "The Great Pensions Scandal" 1 August, 1982.
(3) Bow Paper "The Moral Basis of Conservatism" 1980 P.3.
(4) F.A. Hayek: Law Legislation and Liberty Vol. 1 London 1979 P.3.
(5) See purchase by employees of the National Freight Corporation and tenders for street cleaning in Hammersmith and Fulham and for refuse collection in Birmingham.

INFLATION: APPENDIX 1

100 year value of the Government's pound

One hundred pounds saved in 1884 would now be worth less than four pounds.

Of one hundred pounds lent to the British Government in 1939 only eight pounds would be returned to the investor today.

YEAR	POUND REAL VALUE
1884	100p
1900	113p
1913	98p
1924	56p
1946	48p
1954	33p
1964	25p
1974	13p
1980	5.5p
1984	4p

INFLATION: APPENDIX 2

The value of farm land 1946-1983 "with possession"

Historically investment in land has not produced large returns and there has been an ever decreasing requirement for labour. Inflation however made the hedge of land investment preferable to investment in industry and jobs.

YEAR	£ PER ACRE	% CHANGE
1949	76	
1950	80	+5.2
1951	88	+10
1952	76	−4.5
1953	73	−3.9
1954	75	+2.6
1955	80	+6.6
1956	78	+2.5
1957	73	−6.4
1958	85	+16
1959	101	+18.8
1960	123	+21.7
1961	124	+0.8
1962	134	+8.0
1963	168	+25
1964	214	+27
1965	235	+9.8
1966	242	+2.9
1967	258	+6.6
1968	280	+7.8
1969	299	+6.7
1970	245	**
1971	262	+6.9
1972	596	+127
1973	757	+27
1974	636	−16
1975	539	−15
1976	734	+36
1977	991	+35
1978	1327	+34
1979	1769	+33
1980	1726	−2.4
1981	1729	−
1982	1844	+6.6
1983	2089	+13

Land value growth 1949-1983: 13.3% p.a.
Inflation average 1949-1983: 7.2% p.a.
Real value growth 1949-1983: 6.1% p.a.

INFLATION: APPENDIX 3

The value of Building Society deposits 1946-1983

Few investments have been such a poor protection against inflation as Building Society deposits – the traditional investment of the poor the youngest and the old. While Government profited from inflation, they lost.

YEAR	GROSS INTEREST*	INFLATION	NET
1946	6.48	4.5	2.0
1947	6.36	5.9	0.5
1948	6.36	4.9	1.5
1949	6.36	3.1	3.2
1950	6.36	6.8	−0.4
1951	4.7	9.1	−4.4
1952	4.6	5.8	−1.2
1953	4.5	2.5	2.0
1954	4.5	3.0	1.5
1955	4.7	4.9	−0.2
1956	5.2	4.4	1.2
1957	6.0	3.4	2.6
1958	6.0	1.8	4.2
1959	5.5	0.8	4.7
1960	5.4	2.2	3.2
1961	5.7	3.9	1.8
1962	6.0	3.0	3.0
1963	5.7	2.7	3.0
1964	5.7	4.0	2.7
1965	6.4	4.3	2.1
1966	6.7	3.5	3.2
1967	7.2	2.4	4.8
1968	7.5	5.9	1.6
1969	8.25	4.7	3.4
1970	8.5	7.9	0.6
1971	8.2	9.0	−0.8
1972	8.1	7.7	0.4
1973	9.6	10.6	−1.0
1974	11.0	19.1	−8.0
1975	10.9	24.9	−14.0
1976	10.6	15.1	−5.0
1977	10.6	12.1	−1.5
1978	9.4	8.4	1.0
1979	12.2	17.2	−5.0
1980	15.0	15.1	−0.1
1981	12.8	12.0	0.8
1982	12.1	5.4	5.7
1983	9.6	5.6	4.0

*Year's rate or average rate – grossed up for basic rate tax.

Annual average real return 1946-1983: +0.65% p.a.

PART II

The Failure of Government Intervention

1 Edward Heath and the people of Consett

Between 1945 and 1979 the United Kingdom suffered one of the most dramatic economic declines in the history of the world. From being the richest country in Europe the United Kingdom declined to become the third poorest – richer only than the largely peasant communities of Greece and Ireland. For nearly 40 years the United Kingdom was characterised by economic collectivism. Government, Trade Unions and those corporations large enough to exert political pressure combined to give increasing dominance to Government "analysis" over business responsibility, collectivist decisions over individual choice and interest group power over consumer control.

There were only three periods during this astonishing descent when the cycle of decline could have been arrested. In 1957 MacMillan overruled the wiser counsels of Powell, Thorneycroft and others and set in train the events which led to record unemployment in 1963, the loss of the 1964 election and the long period of Government domination of economic life throughout the 1960's and 1970's. In 1979 Mrs Thatcher at last succeeded in bringing about the necessary revolution. In 1970 however Mr Heath had started on a similar path only to take fright at the exposure – in the form of over one million unemployed – of the long suppressed inadequacies of British industry and successive Governments which had protected companies from the consequences of those inadequacies.

In 1972 Mr Heath returned to the post war "tripartite consensus" of Government, Trade Unions and large corporations whose centralised and irresponsible claims to economic wisdom were financed by relieving the old, the young and the less privileged of their savings. In 1979 Mrs Thatcher discarded that dishonourable consensus and required at long last that consensus which is the basis of a democratic society – the economic sovereignty of the consumer and the political sovereignty of the voter.

On 20th January 1985 Mr Heath continued his 10 year vendetta against Mrs Thatcher and asked in the Sunday Times "What do we tell the people of Consett?" Consett is a town in North West Durham where, following the loss of the British Steel plant in 1980 unemployment rose to over 25%. Mr Heath called, as is his wont, for "investment in public expenditure for the benefit of the community as a whole".

The writer, having lived in Consett for over 20 years was all too aware of the ludicrous nature of past "public investment" in the town and was anxious to warn of the siren voices of the left and right wing Establishments who see in any misfortune a chance to make political capital and in any economic decline the prospect of personal political advancement! The claims of such political figures are all the more ludicrous when one compares their personal ignorance with the business acumen, technical skills and real work experience of those they wish to "help".

For over one hundred years Consett was a successful entrepreneurial steel town. Before the first world war Consett was the world's largest steel producer – thanks to the initiative and marketing of the Consett Iron Company. In the 1950's the Conservatives re privatised the steel industry after post war nationalisation and in 1967, in response to declining steel production, to "preserve jobs" and for ideological reasons the Labour Government again nationalised the industry. Control passed to London. Governments invested massively in the British Steel Corporation. Consett became an outpost of a declining State run empire. 13 years later 4,000 jobs disappeared overnight when the Consett works were closed.

The post war history of Consett and the steel company was a microcosm of what was happening nationwide throughout British Industry. Nationalisation, Government subsidy and intervention preserved and collectivised business for "social" reasons. Outdated forms of production, assets and jobs were subsidised long past their natural lives. More and more steel towns like Consett, shipping towns like Newcastle, coal areas like Durham became artificial Government subsidised shells relying increasingly on political patronage from the distant and ignorant (often socialist) London establishment.

The entrepreneurs, the trained workers, the educated middle class left the area for the South, for Australia, America, Germany, Rhodesia, – in fact anywhere where skills were appreciated and the enterprising were lauded and rewarded.

In the vacuum remaining Socialism was happily ensconced in corrupt town halls living – economically and ideologically – from the political largesse of regional grants and local public sector dominated economies. The local businessman was derided and his needs were sacrificed to please some persuasive London based property developer, merchant banker or young American executive (sent to cut his commercial teeth on some high risk marginal venture, the cost of which was borne principally by Her Majesty's Government and to which the commitment of the corporation was correspondingly "discounted"!)

And what of Mr Heath's record? His own money printing boom in 1972/73, resulting in the 25% inflation of 1974/75, was responsible for the artificial boost to unsustainable businesses. The *Government* stimulated demand gave the declining industries – steel, ships, coal – on which the North East was already too heavily dependent, a further shot of morphine. Outdated plant, loss making investment, poor working practices, poor management and rapacious unions were preserved. In Consett few managers worked as they had in the days of private enterprise, workers rarely worked a full shift, night shifts were often paid slumber and foremen and skilled workers went back to unskilled jobs where the pay was higher!

Skilled workers, capital and valuable assets which could have found more profitable employment elsewhere were hoarded in loss making pursuits. Stocks were built too high, borrowing rose too high and new forms of supply and innovation were (apparently) not required in the face of Mr Heath's artificial demand.

What Governments and Mr Heath never seem to ask themselves is how the regions of Britain were ever wealthy enough in the first place to attract the populations which they now seek to subsidise into loss making dependence on the rest of Britain. What of the magnificent industrial achievements of the Clyde, Tyne and Mersey whose people are now the verbal cannon fodder in the vaccuous rhetoric of politicians on their ambitious road (South) to Westminster?

Those areas were the cradle of the world's first industrial revolution and produced some of our greatest entrepreneurs –

Swann, Parsons, Armstrong, Stevenson, Arkwright. All they had was their geographic position, ingenuity and the freedom to trade – very much like the Hong Kongs and Singapores of the post war period. They created whole industries and, by comparison to the landed poverty and dependence which preceded them, unparalleled wealth for their workers. What these regions did not have of course was a massive State apparatus investing in commercially unconstrained nationalised industries and directing, through fiscal largesse, the investment of private industry.

Mr Heath's diagnosis is wrong and Consett does not need his compassion. The value of compassion is often in inverse relation to the self gratification of the compassionate – and Mr Heath seems to glory too much in his compassion! He seems to have learned nothing, but perhaps that is because, unlike the people of Consett, Mr Heath has not suffered the consequences of *his* previous actions!!

2 The United Kingdom Energy Industry State Failure and Market Future (1985)

"Brilliantly argued"
Financial Times Energy Economist

INTRODUCTION

Within the Department of Energy Government Ministers have direct responsibility for the largest of all monopoly nationalised assets. Coal, Gas, Electricity and Nuclear Power constitute a large part of GDP, are central in the chain of industrial production and harbour within them the most valuable materials, capital and human skills utilised with neither commercial constraints nor incentives in loss making (coal) or 'profit' making (gas and electricity) industries.

After six years of a Government devoted to market principles not one significant area of our energy industry has been returned to the commercial disciplines of the market place and therefore to *real* public control. Even the sale of the British Gas Corporation seems likely to result in a non-competitive structure with a spread of shareholders so wide as to provide few commercial constraints on a management accustomed to State backed sovereignty over consumers and competitors.

As in other industrial sectors where privatisation has been achieved the Government seems to have more regard for the receipts from a privatised offspring of the State than for the true purpose of privatisation: to return what have been erroneously called 'public assets' to the *genuine* control of the public in a competitive market.

Government receipts from privatisation are being treated in the public accounts as a reduction in public expenditure rather

73

than as what they truly are – the financing of expenditure. Merely to privatise a monopoly, however regulated, in order to maximise Exchequer revenue is contrary to two important principles.

1. Capital receipts are being used to finance current expenditure.
2. The purpose of reduced taxes is to return spending power to the public who by their responsible spending decisions will force producers to find responsible and efficient uses for the assets they own. If taxes are reduced by the launch of a monopoly then the public have no more *control* than before privatisation. Their increased net income will be extracted by a private monopoly and will find its way back to the Exchequer as a windfall tax!

This paper emphasises the true purpose of privatisation, describes the State dominated structure of the UK energy industry and lists the failures, contradictions and market distortions which have resulted. The ideal structure for an energy industry responsible to consumers is described but, conscious of the probably sale of BGC in its present (defective) form, the paper proposes a surrogate market structure and specific restrictions on a privatised BGC. The proposed *Office of Energy Regulation* would be obliged to monitor and regulate not just BGC but also the remaining nationalised energy industries and their relations with the new private gas corporation.

THE PURPOSE OF PRIVATISATION

The principal purpose of privatisation is *not* the removal of borrowing from the definition of the 'PSBR'. It is *not* to raise funds for the Exchequer. It is not even to put assets into private sector *control*. The principal purpose is to ensure that assets are owned by those who have the incentive to seek commercial returns on their use but who are constrained by competing commercial enterprises and therefore the freedom of consumers to 'take their custom elsewhere'.

Within such a structure of *ownership* it is therefore the sovereign *consumer* who *controls* the use of assets. When the State owns industry it has the power to exclude competitors by law and to use taxpayers money to cover the losses which indicate their failure to serve customers. State ownership, unlike private ownership *does mean* control.

The degree to which private ownership is responsible and efficient depends crucially on the structure of the market in which a company operates. A monopoly will continue even in private hands to exploit consumers and waste national assets. A private company with assets and power acquired during its existence as a publicly financed monopoly and with special advantages (privileged knowledge of competitors assets or Government protection from takeover) can upset the balance of responsibility and reward in an industrial sector, and undermine competitors. The resulting concentration of power reduces or eliminates consumer control.

THE FAILURE OF THE UK ENERGY INDUSTRY

The Energy market, despite widespread myths to the contrary, is like any other market. In order to meet the needs of consumers, producers must have clear signals of price, cost and available resources. Changes in supply and demand and in the behaviour of producers and consumers occur *at the margin*. In other words, it is not necessary for supply to fall to nothing before a change in price will bring about a change in demand, and it is not necessary for demand to double before a change in price will stimulate supply. Small changes in any variable will effect a compensating change elsewhere to bring the market back to a balance at the price which people will pay.

In the case of energy *price* is crucial. Unlike manufactured goods which only "exist" after they have been produced, oil, gas and other extracted minerals exist in nature but only exist economically by reference to their price. We talk of "economically recoverable reserves" – that is the price at which a certain amount of oil or gas can be extracted and yield a return to the producer. If the price rises the definition of reserves rises – overnight, as it were – without any work on the part of those who own the assets. If the price falls then the economically recoverable reserves fall.

The price which acts as signal of the very *existence* of minerals *must* be a true market price. The true price can only be determined spontaneously in a market whose competing producers deal with free rational consumers. Any attempt to control the market by a Government or monopoly will immediately produce an *artificial* price. This in turn produces an *artificial* picture of the amount of oil or gas in "economic existence". As we have seen in the case of the nationalised energy monopolies in Britain, State ownership and non market, Government imposed prices have distorted national economic decisions with the result that:

1. The BGC monopsony paid low prices to domestic producers and high prices to foreign (Norwegian) producers. This stimulated production in Norway and reduced production in the UK, boosting the Norwegian Government's tax take and reducing our own.
2. The monopsony controlled low gas prices to producers were partially passed on to gas consumers. Gas therefore bought a very high share of the domestic heating market at the cost of coal and electricity. Since this was done on the basis of prices which did not reflect the long run cost of gas, consumers were misled into irrational long term investments.
3. On the assumption that UK gas reserves were low (naturally the economically recoverable reserves were defined in terms of the controlled artificially low price) BGC wished to commit to a long term contract to import Norwegian gas. This would have meant an enormous cost to the balance of payments and large foregone Exchequer revenue from taxation of *domestic* gas fields. The Government rightly prevented this.
4. The distortion of the gas price and its dominance in domestic consumer markets made rational commercial decisions in coal, nuclear and electricity markets more difficult. Industrial gas sales were at even lower prices (between 1975 and 1984 an average of 55% of domestic gas prices) even though gas claimed to be a premium fuel for high value added production.
5. Since UK gas prices to producers have risen to approach market levels domestic recoverable reserves have risen substantially – by far more than the volume of gas which has been imported from Norway since 1978! Why, then, did the United Kingdom import that gas at considerable cost?

Remaining recoverable proven and probable reserves of gas on UK Continental Shelf:

31 December 1980	38.9 trillion cu ft
31 December 1984	46.8 trillion cu ft
Total cumulative production to 31/12/80	13.4 trillion cu ft
Total cumulative production to 31/12/84	17.8 trillion cu ft
Therefore gas found between 1980 and 1984	12.3 trillion cu ft
Gas imported from Frigg 1977 to 1985:	3.2 trillion cu ft

6. The failure to market price gas has meant massive flaring of gas associated with oil production. Since 1977 an average of 12 million cubic metres per day have been burned away in the UK sector of the North Sea.
7. The UK Electricity Industry has been confronted not only by artificially low priced gas but was also required to buy coal from the NCB at above market prices. This subsidy allowed the coal industry to continue mining coal at a cost far in excess of what any rational customer would pay.
8. Special taxes on fuel oil have also served as an indirect subsidy to coal.
9. Government subsidy of nuclear power (through monopoly non commercial ownership) has probaby artificially reduced the natural role of coal as an electricity generator and made the "commercial" price of coal even more difficult to ascertain.
10. Import controls have kept coal prices artificially high. Export controls have kept gas prices artificially low.
11. Oil prices – for so long artificially controlled by an international cartel – competed with coal, gas and nuclear which were artificially controlled by State monopolies. Now that oil prices are falling State ownership prevents the automatic readjustment of competing energy sources on a rational basis.

12. UK gas and electricity are – unlike in Europe – not subject to VAT. This is a reflection of the "tax" which the UK Government extracts by over-pricing some fuels and losses incurred by State owned energy industries (a loss by the State is a tax on the people). In Europe independent private and regional ownership of energy produces better use of assets and overt, visible taxation by VAT not least because the producers, consumers and taxing authorities are separate and therefore counterbalancing entities.

13. The promotion of nuclear power by Government is similar to the control of gas prices by BGC. Since there are no constraints from commercial shareholders, competitors or free consumers, there is no objective and spontaneous determination of price, cost, reserves, and the opportunity cost of alternatives. In addition the overriding power of such State decisions destroys such market signals for genuine market operators. Where nuclear power generation is the subject of rational commercial decisions (USA) investment is now nil.

14. The environmental dangers of nuclear power are (like UK energy in general) totally outside the control of those in danger – consumers. Where Government owns assets, it controls every aspect of their use and is not open to independent safety controls. Where the private sector owns assets consumers are controllers of their commercial use and Government is a check on environmental safety.

15. Nationalised coal, gas and electricity industries incur varying costs depending on which part of the country they supply to. But these cost differences are not reflected in prices. Therefore those areas which are close to coal (Northern England) gas (Eastern England and N.W. England) are in effect taxed to subsidise relatively prosperous areas like the South West and South East (from where the nationalised energy industries are controlled!)

16. The lack of commercial constraints and incentives for UK nationalised energy industries has meant a lack of any commercial approach to energy conservation. Two mechanisms are required for rational and efficient conservation: market pricing to encourage consumers to consider conservation and private commercial energy producers who will consider investment in consumer *conservation* as a rational alternative to high capital expenditure on energy

78

supply. The private energy utilities in the USA on occasion even offer free credit for insulation rather than invest in more production capacity.

An energy market based on Government price control and subsidies and State owned industries provides none of these constraints and opportunities and the UK's record on conservation bears testimony to this:

	Annual Average Rate of Change 1973-83	
Japan	-3.6	
USA	-2.5	
Germany	-2.8	
UK		-2.3

17. As in other Government controlled markets the most important failure is the loss of overt costs and prices. BGC does not publish gas tariffs. It does not publish gas import prices. Government itself gives no reasons for the award or non award of oil and gas exploration licences. These *covert* systems give arbitrary power and prevent rational actions by responsible operators in the energy market.

THE IDEAL STRUCTURE FOR UK ENERGY

The privatisation of the BGC offers an opportunity to establish an *energy* industry (rather than a gas or coal or electricity industry) responsible to shareholders and consumers alike. Only a market structure undistorted by Government controls and monopoly ownership can identify and price resources, identify and respond to the needs of consumers and optimise the use of (scarce) national resources.

No energy source has any intrinsic value. It merely has a use the price for which will change in response to real need and present and perceived supply. Both conservation and long term planning (often thought to be the prerogative of Government and not amenable to purely commercial activity) are in fact *only* effectively achieved through market pricing and commercial activity.

Conservation is a rational response by consumers to a situation of actual and expected shortage as reflected in a high price. If the price is low it means either there is no shortage in which case "conservation" would be irrational or Government or some other monopoly is preventing prices from signalling a shortage. If the latter is the case then further distortion by Government inspired "conservation" subsidy will not help. The original distortion need only be removed.

Long term planning is not ony possible in the private sector it is more widely and more successfully practised than in the public sector. From the decision to explore for oil and gas to the end of the life of a discontinued field is typically 15 or 20 years. Such decisions occur every year in many competing commercial companies and the price of failure is the loss of shareholder funds. If a State owned *industry* makes only *one* decision about the *whole* UK market in 20 years' time then of course the results can be catastrophic – as we can see with the very large excess capacity in the coal and electricity industries. But the dangers of failure are very large when few decisions are taken by commercially unconstrained producers in a monopoly position. Failure is a consequence of the very structure of the industry. In a competitive market there are many competing decisions and forecasts and, most important of all, *market pricing* to define real supply, real demand and real reserves.

There are no logical or commercial barriers to privatisation in the energy sector. Indeed, there are already limited private-sector inputs and competitive elements.

Oil is market-priced with many producers (including foreign) selling to a myriad consumers in a highly competitive market. Private corporations may produce and sell electricity.

North Sea gas producers may sell direct to commercial consumers, utilising the gas network as common carrier. There are many private coal producers who sell to the NCB (albeit only 1% of total production) and open-cast mining is largely contracted out by the NCB to private companies.

In the case of the coal industry there is no "natural monopoly" network so there is even less to prevent privatisation. Even the fact that an industry is loss-making should not prevent its sale, since it is of equal value for a Government to forego a loss as to realise a profit-making asset. Given the right environment, investors may be prepared to bid more (relative to capital value) for a loss-making concern, since they may see outstanding opportunities for a financial turnround.

The steps to privatisation of the coal industry should be: the removal of import restrictions and fiscal burdens on competing fuels, the withdrawal of NCB powers to license and price private coal production, the regionalising of coal pricing within the NCB and, finally, the establishment of competing regional coal companies ready for the introduction of private capital. The companies would then be privatised as *energy* companies.

In the electricity industry, the existing area boards (possibly reorganised into seven or eight comparable regions) could be established as separate entities allowed to bid for supply and fuel input across regional boundaries.

The national grid would remain for the present in public hands as a common carrier and the new regional companies would choose, depending on their commercial interest, their own mix of competitive – cross-regional sales.

Large independent suppliers could sell direct to large consumers, utilising the national grid and paying a tariff, or they could sell to the regional electricity company, although it may prove beneficial for groups of households, especially on new estates, to form a negotiating group, taking advantage of bulk-supply terms.

The gas industry, unlike electricity, where there are many potential onshore suppliers, obtains most of its supplies from offshore, principally from the North Sea (UK and Norway). It can be privatised with the Regional Boards the basis for competing private sector distribution companies (see below).

It is important to remember that energy is the marketable commodity, not oil, gas or coal. The decentralised and commercialised structure of the energy industries will rapidly lead to cooperation, mergers and take-overs among the various regional companies specialising in one fuel and genuine energy companies will emerge with no outdated attachment to any particular fuel, but with a commercial incentive to provide energy to all consumers.

There is no reason why the shape of the industry should not be based on a variety of commercial enterprises whose local inputs and marketing opportunities as energy generators or distributors will break down the rigidities of monopoly standard pricing for a standard product in a protected environment.

The nuclear industry, after nearly 40 years of costly and commercially unconstrained investment to supply another State monopoly – electricity – still manages to produce only 5% of the nation's energy needs. The billions of pounds of public money spent on nuclear power *may* be very rational and in the interests of consumers but, being a public sector, tax payer subsidised monopoly we have no way of knowing this, and neither has the Government.

Given the Government's welcome scepticism about the wisdom of other State controlled commercial enterprises its devotion to the State Nuclear Industry is somewhat puzzling.

The privatisation of British Gas (or the profitability of the coal and electricity industries prior to *their* privatisation) cannot be jeopardised by applying a completely different and contradictory set of criteria to the Nuclear Industry.

THE POLITICAL DIMENSION

Despite the demonstration of State failure in the Energy Industry there is admittedly a general impression that private ownership may mean fewer jobs and less "public" control. And yet Government control of coal has meant the loss of over half a million jobs since the War while there have been equally dramatic job losses in those industries – steel, engineering and other high energy consumers – as gas, coal and electricity prices have risen under Government "control".

Commercial ownership in a freer market will lead to many more uses for coal (for gas, chemicals, vehicle fuel) and there are excellent prospects for jobs in Combined Heat & Power projects which will consume coal. Conservation investment by private energy utilities have created many jobs in the USA and would do so in the UK given the commercial possibilities of a less controlled energy market.

Many political decisions in the coal, electricity and nuclear industries have prevented rather than encouraged the creation of jobs. All the *one fuel* energy utilities – nuclear, coal, gas – are prone to the risk of over-reliance on one form of production. In energy companies, workers can be switched from one fuel to another and from production to sales, thus making their employment more secure. The proposed, more rational commercial *energy* companies will provide more secure and profitable jobs *throughout* the energy industry.

THE PRIVATISATION OF
THE BRITISH GAS CORPORATION

The purpose of privatisation is to return effective control of commercial assets to the consumer by allowing those with a commercial incentive to maximise the use of assets to compete freely in the market place.

In the case of the British Gas Corporation this can only be achieved by splitting the Corporation into 3 separate parts. The offshore production interests should be auctioned off. The pipeline network should, *pro tem,* remain a public sector utility and the Regional Gas Boards should be privatised as separate and competing commercial companies with no restrictions as to their commercial activities in other energy sources. These proposals would prevent many of the problems of monopoly which can only be otherwise addressed by a regulatory authority with a very complex set of guidelines.

The Government should ideally halt the process of privatising BGC until there has been a complete evaluation of the above proposals. However, in the absence of any such reassessment of the form of privatisation, there therefore remains a regulatory authority for the following structure of the Gas Industry, privatised in its present form.

In the absence of a competitive structure the Government is obliged to devise a surrogate market mechanism which will prevent exploitation of consumers, minimise distortions in the energy market and provide both incentives and discipline for the British Gas Corporation.

THE REGULATORY AUTHORITY

It is generaly accepted that the monitoring of a powerful monopoly can only be carried out by an authority outside the Department of Energy. There can be no detailed understanding of the problems and opportunities of the Gas Industry without knowledge of and the ability to control other State energy industries with which the privatised gas industry will compete. We therefore require not just a gas regulatory board but an OFFICE OF ENERGY REGULATION ("OFFER").

In the absence of a complete market energy structure the State as continuing "shareholder" in coal, nuclear and electricity cannot be allowed to manipulate and subsidise the gas industry's competitors outside the disciplines of "OFFER". The Energy industry regulator will also prevent the manipulation of energy prices by Government as a means of raising revenue for the Exchequer or – by suppressing prices – buying votes at a

General Election.

The Gas Consumer Council as the defender of consumer interests in the face of a nationalised monopoly will in future have its interests represented by "OFFER" into which *some* of the Council may be absorbed.

Since the principles of energy market regulation are almost identical with those applied regularly in other industries "OFFER" should share offices, facilities and back-up staff with the Monopolies and Mergers Commission, whilst maintaining a separate identity.

RESTRICTIONS ON PRIVATISED GAS INDUSTRY

A. So long as the coal, nuclear and electricity industries remain in State control, restricted by statute to their fuel sources and products and their assets protected from purchase by commercial corporations, then for so long must the British Gas Corporation be restricted to the role of gas supplier. Its present position as offshore producer must be allowed to wither away as its present fields deplete. By permitting BGC to retain both its offshore producer role and its position as quasi-monopsonist purchaser of gas from other offshore producers, the scope for manipulation of competing producers is enormous.

Such scope is further increased by BGC's access to privileged information about the exploration results of other companies in the North Sea and the ability to "transfer price" from production to gas distribution companies.

Hungry as BGC will be to acquire offshore oil and gas companies, its power to delay or refuse gas purchase could substantially reduce the share price of those companies to its advantage. BGC must not be permitted to acquire other oil and gas companies.

There need be no restriction on the purchase of other gas supply utilities.

B. The 3 distinct operations of BGC and the Regional Boards should be required by Statute to prepare separate accounts.

C. The clause in the Enterprise Act which restricts purchase of gas from companies other than BGC to a minimum of 25,000 therms per annum must be removed.

THE GAS LEVY

A. The gas levy must continue. Revenue from it has already reached its peak and the gas contracts to which it applies will gradually wither away by the 1990s. The returns to BGC which are taxed by the levy arise out of gas contracts exempt from PRT and concluded in the early stages of gas development in the Southern North Sea.

B. The Stock Exchange cannot reasonably object to such a levy. Investment in television and oil companies which suffer similar "excess profit" levies are not noticeably restricted. Government should of course be more interested in removing the source of the excess profit rather than taxing it and in the case of BGC privatisation the cause is being tackled and the source of the levy will automatically be rectified.

C. The two main reasons for maintaining the Gas Levy are: *Firstly*, that it prevents the privatised BGC from obtaining a *cash windfall* with which it could be an even less restrained predator of other independent oil and gas companies (the nature of gas supply requires little working capital so cash is not required for that purpose). *Secondly*, the capital value of future BGC profits *without* the Levy are likely to be heaviy discounted by the Stock Market since only two years of such an "advantage" (i.e. to the next election!) can be calculated with any certainty. The Government would therefore forego substantial future revenues for a very small increase in capital value today.

EXPORTS, IMPORTS AND PRICE CONTROLS

A. There should be no restrictions on exports. However, BGC must not be allowed to discriminate against domestic producers by offering a higher price for imports. Exports, or at least their genuine *possibility* will ensure that UK producers receive market prices for exploration and production in UK waters. They will therefore maximise the value to the UK of gas resources and optimise the pace of exploration activity. (During the 1970s the absence of such market constraints led BGC to reduce UK production and import instead from Norway whose own exploration and production we financed!) A privatised BGC, paying market prices for gas, will be less able to underprice to consumers and provide unfair competition for alternative energy sources – including the Government's own energy industries!

B. There will be no need to control the British Gas Corporation's capital expenditure or return on assets. The corporation's private sector shareholders, while seeking commercial returns, will be constrained by free consumers and producers able to obtain genuine market prices for their product (see A above). The corporation will therefore be able to maximise its returns *only* by providing an efficient service to consumers.

C. *Predatory pricing* by BGC remains a threat to the energy market, even in the context of market pricing. By the very size of balance sheet and access to large volumes of gas on historically low priced contracts, the new corporation could "raid" targeted sectors of the domestic and particularly industrial markets.

  The threat to *overpricing* is largely met by the need to pay market prices to producers and to maintain market share, but the threat of *underpricing* must be met by not allowing prices to fall blow the long run marginal cost. Alternatively BGC could be required by "OFFER" to sustain any price cut for a minimum period, thus making any predatory (underpricing) element a costly experience.

D. *Relating gas prices to inflation or even oil prices* is neither necessary, given the more natural market constraints above, nor wise. Inflation is a general indicator of the value of *money* unlikely to bear much relation to the *real* cost changes in a specific industry like gas. Oil prices, while giving a better indication of energy market prices, are nevertheless inadequate. Oil prices are short term and international while real gas price movements are for long term contracts in largely regional markets.

  BGC must be required to publish a gas transmission tariff – in "pounds per cubic metre mile", the level of which must be vetted by "OFFER".

CONSERVATION AND STATE ENERGY CORPORATIONS

For energy utilities, whether privately or State owned, *conser-*

vation investment is a valid commercial alternative to very large *production* investment in plant, materials and infrastructure. In the USA where there is more regionally and locally based *commercial* competition, conservation investment is a natural alternative. In State owned, non commercial enterprises this has proved not to be the case, partly because of the structure of non commercial ownership and partly because Government has underpriced energy so that energy savings seem not to be in the consumers' interest.

Recent "market" gas price rises and the privatisation of BGC will remove these impediments as far as the *gas* market is concerned. Any decision by BGC between production or conservation investment will be "rational". However, BGC will be competing with State owned, controlled and subsidised Coal and Electricity industries where monopoly profits or subsidised losses permit "irrational" decisions. *These* industries must therefore be forced by Government to consider conservation investment as an alternative to production investment.

By the same token, Coal, Nuclear and Electricity could use their privileged positions in the non commercial sector to "predatory price" against BGC. This too must be the subject of monitoring by the new regulatory authority, "OFFER".

CONCLUSION

The sale of a State monopoly to the commercial sector, rather than the sale of its assets, involves a complex set of regulations even when the rest of the energy market is commercially constrained by competition and free consumers. When, in addition, the State will retain control of much of energy production and sale, the restrictions on anti-competitive practices must be all the more rigorous.

The above set of proposals for regulation of the energy market following the privatisation of British Gas Corporation must be taken as a whole. The removal of any one constraint can invalidate the effectiveness of the others.

3 The Businessman's supply creates the Economists demand

We are accustomed to hearing the monotonous drone of Government critics appealing for an "injection of demand" in order to stimulate economic growth. Those who express such opinions usually have little conception of the business process – even though, paradoxically, many of them are engaged in it. Unfortunately their influence has grown in proportion to the spread of Government control over economic life and we must fear that the economists' demand for demand may result in supply.

In the exchange of goods and services there are five elements which could be the object for analysis: the good or service itself, its price (which will include the element "cost") the customer, the amount supplied and the amount sold. Conclusions resulting from the analysis of these elements will depend crucially on the cultural and occupational characteristics of the analyst. Much will also depend on the degree of personal responsibiity the analyst has for the consequences of actions based on his analysis.

Traditionally those who have influenced Government action or the actions of large private sector institutions are economists, political scientists, social analysts or business planners, steeped in economists' methods. They have a natural propensity to analyse and base their models on that which can be measured and presented in aggregate statistical form. Those statistical forms, since they are compiled for the use of economists, reflect a preoccupation with the number of goods produced and "demanded", average prices paid and changes in nominal prices.

The economist's study of changes in aggregate nominal prices reflects a pre-occupation with inflation, that is changes in the value of *money*, not changes in relative real prices. The relationship between nominal and real price changes is at least measurable but there is a similar (non measurable) difference between nominal goods and services and real goods and services, in the sense of their nominal and real *utility*. The crucial "ratio" in business is the ratio of price to utility. The number and formal description of the goods is not as important as their utility to the customer. The degree of utility of any goods or service is a function of so many facets that the measurement of price and a purely functional description ("car", "handbag", "banking") are woefully inadequate to characterise its value. Similarly on the other side of the exchange there are so many different types of customer and so many different requirements of the same people at different *times* and in different circumstances that to characterise that as "demand" is at best dilettante and at worst a distortion of the truth.

It is the sophisticated task of marketeers and entrepreneurs to sift the enormous complexity of individual and group preferences, to identify needs (often long before they are perceived by customers) and then to value a new product or the smallest change in the characteristics of an existing product. There is, most significantly, no conception of a *fixed* anything. Costs, prices, supply, demand are all dynamic and most important they do not change in any predictable manner. Indeed if such business variables were easily predictable there would be little role for business judgement, little scope for profit and no requirement for entrepreneurship. Entrepreneurs are essentially optimists. They believe they can *change* preferences for their advantage, they can *reduce* costs, they can find "a new way" and they can stimulate demand through innovation – and they are right!

The elements of economic activity which concern the entrepreneur are product quality, customer needs and real (ie relative!) price changes. They are not conducive to statistical aggregation, exact definition or "scientific" analysis. They are not within the grasp or experience of economics or social analysts, nor, I am afraid, have they much relevance for corporate planners in the sterilised towers of large corporations.

We can categorise the elements of economic activity which concern businessmen and economists:

Businessman	*Economist*
Customer needs	Aggregate demand
Product quality	Aggregate supply
Real price changes	Nominal price changes
Motivation	Results
Causes	Symptoms
Change (real)	Change (statistical)
Future possibilities	Historical facts

The essence of business is uncertainty, not knowledge. Information does of course increase the probability of business success but the relative judgements of individual businessmen are more important than graphs or historical statistics. Indeed in business the greatest rewards accrue to those who buck conventional wisdom and economic analysis and strike out on their own where competitors fear to tread. The true businessman does not respond to measured demand for existing products for he sees that many others are competing at ever lower margins for stale and easily predictable patterns of supply. A good indicator of the imminent decline of a profitable line would be its classification, measurement and exposure to chart analysis by economists!

Economists and other social analysts are not concerned with the preferences of customers, the characteristics of the product or the real burden on individual consumers. Rather they are concerned with the measurement and (crude) classification of aggregates and movements in averages. Such activities enjoy a scientific aura of respectability and the mere process of aggregation and neatly printing statistics presents a seemingly tangible and factual basis for decisions.

For business the anticipation of individual and social behaviour is the key to success. To detect potential changes accurately involves a close relationship with customers, their moods, finances and needs. It also requires a complete lack of bias or personal prejudice about products and consumers – a refreshing contrast to the often narrow and vitriolic exchange of academic abuse by economists!

The studies of an economist make such intimate involvement with reality neither possible nor – given the nature of his "arms length" analytical brief – necessary. It is the brief he is given by Government which is often the source of pseudo-scientific results and the cause of bad decisions based on those results. The profession has fallen in public esteem, not because their activity was redundant but because the institutions which bought their expertise began to extend their aegis of control to detailed business decisions. They increasingly made business decisions on behalf of businessmen, financial decisions on behalf of individuals and centralised decisions on behalf of previously decentralised organisations. Their failure to define the areas of their true competence ultimately devalued not only their own activities but the professional activities of their economists.

There is no better example of the gulf between economic analysis and business reality than the failure of Government to understand the relationship between supply and demand. Among non businessmen it is a common assumption (independent of but compounded by Keynesian influence) that the production of goods or services followed demonstrated demand for them. In fact, apart from satisfying basic hunger and thirst, demand tends to be stimulated by supply. Even basic provision of shelter and warmth in primitive societies were not "demanded". The first man to crawl into a cave and cover himself with leaves took advantage of his own ability to create a new form of *supply*. His own "demand" for a cave and leaves was only crystallised and determinable as such after it had been "supplied". If this were true for a primitive non trading society then it is doubly true today when so many rely on *others* to identify and provide goods and services.

The purpose of business is *not* to (a) raise revenue by (b) meeting demand and (c) increasing production – although this is exactly how Governments, Trade Unions and many economists see the process. The purpose of business is to create value – and hence wealth for shareholders – by increasing the utility of goods and services in relation to their price. This could in fact mean the opposite of a, b, and c. It could mean cutting production of existing goods and ignoring demand for a product in order to introduce a completely new product in smaller amounts with lower costs and lower revenue but of greater utility to the customer and hence of higher profitability to the producer.

The preoccupation of the economist with the symptoms of *aggregate* business activity has led Government to base policies on the stimulation of those symptoms. Lack of jobs and declining wealth have been traced to lack of "demand" and so "demand" has been stimulated through the injection of money into the economy. *Real* demand (as opposed to money demand) is of course unlikely to be affected merely by the availability of more money since real demand is a function of changes in the quality, cost and pattern of supply. Lack of demand and under-utilised capacity arise not through the actions of some "deus ex machina". They arise because businessmen's ability to carry out these changes have been blunted by Government subsidy, price distortion and the resultant perpetuation of outdated forms of supply.

There are few gulfs in society greater than that between the business trained entrepreneur and the scientifically trained economist. The change in their respective social positions in Britain during the 20th Century has reflected an apparent triumph of knowledge over action and Government over business. There should be no gulf between Government and economics on the one hand and business on the other. For what is the purpose of Government but to provide a service? And what is the purpose of economics but to study and understand the lessons of business?

The extent of the United Kingdom's economic decline – so eloquently chronicled and classified by economists – is testimony to the failure of Government and economics to define their roles and understand the strengths of the businessman. We have become a nation of people who know everything but can do nothing.

The longer the Government can resist the economists demand for demand the sooner we will capitalise on the ability of the businessman to supply.

4   Income, Wealth and Capital Taxation

INTRODUCTION

The purpose of this paper is to review the rates and structure of Capital Transfer Tax in the light of what actually constitutes "wealth". There is much confusion in the public mind about what "wealth" is and this confusion has manifested itself in tax and welfare legislation.

Firstly, the paper will define what is not wealth by reference to the amount of capital required to sustain an independently financed individual in the lifestyle of those who do not work but whose real level of benefits are sustained by the state. Secondly, the paper will suggest that the broad principle applied by the Government to other taxes (minimising distortions through reliefs and allowances and reductions in tax rates) should be applied to Capital Transfer Tax.

THE BIAS AGAINST CAPITAL

Capital is foregone expenditure of "stored income". It can be stored out of past income (savings) or it can be stored out of future income (by borrowing). Wherever there is an annual income there is correspondingly an amount of capital to produce that income.

It is assumed by many that those with large capital assets enjoy a large income while those who enjoy large incomes have no wealth. Yet today, many of those with the largest capital (houses, farms and other low yielding assets) have low incomes, while many of those with little capital have the highest incomes. In times of inflation there are many ways that those with high incomes can accumulate capital while there are few ways for someone with capital but little income to even maintain (never mind add to) capital. It is much easier to borrow against future income than against present capital, not least since inflation relieves the borrower of the burden of his debt while robbing the lender of the value of his capital. Under such circumstances, power depends on the regularity of income and certainly not on the ownership of capital.

It is not surprising that, following a period of increasing dominance of the state, wealth today is more a function of pieces of paper representing government and trade union contracts "guaranteeing" income than of capital investment in competitive markets.

The bias against capital ownership and in favour of income ownership is reflected in taxation and welfare legislation:

(a) the level of capital below which people qualify for many benefits is far lower than the capital value of the income those benefits represent;

(b) for many years, inflation "gains" on capital were taxed while government employees and pensioners' incomes were index linked: there was no similar guarantee for the value of capital from which a pensioner derives his or her income in the private sector;

(c) if an asset is sold at a gain, then that gain is taxed even if the proceeds are re-invested. The man who has made a capital gain is taxed on his ability to make the gain and taxed again on income from that gained capital! The man who improves his job is taxed on his increased *income* but not on the "gain" of a better job;

(d) while it is possible to set house loan interest (up to a loan of £30,000) against income tax, it is not possible to offset it against tax on capital gains.

Capital taxes are based on the assumption that some are excessively "wealthy" and that some of the wealth might therefore be justifiably removed by government. In order to determine what is not an excessive amount of wealth, we must compare the earnings of people who have income entitlement but no capital with those who have capital and must live from the income. Accordingly, we consider below the earnings of an unemployed man with a wife and two children, and a retired couple. Neither couple work but society rightly expects there to be, somewhere, capital which will yield an income sufficient to keep them, if necessary, indefinitely.

LONG-RUN RETURNS ON CAPITAL

In order to determine how much capital is required for a given long-term income which will compensate for inflation we must see what the typical real returns on capital have been over a period of years. Whatever that yield has been will indicate what capital we shall require to sustain a given real future income.

Since it would undoubtedly be foolish to invest in only one kind of asset for the stability of long term income, let us assume that the capital we require is a diversified portfolio of equities, gilts, building society deposits, and land.

Equities have proved a better investment than gilts or building society deposits in times of inflation, and even in non-inflationary times they are likely to keep pace with general economic success. Companies can of course go bankrupt!

Gilt-edged stock – government fixed-interest securities – will maintain their *nominal* value (governments don't normally go bankrupt) and provide a stable nominal income, unlike equities whose income can fluctuate considerably. Unlike equities, however, there is a real risk that neither income nor capital will keep pace with inflation.

Building society deposits will maintain their nominal value and like gilt-edged stock, are less risky – at least in non-inflationary times – than equity investment. In addition, their interest rate varies (unlike gilts, which are fixed) and should therefore have a better chance of matching inflation *in income terms*. However, if interest paid is say, 10% and inflation 5%, only 5%

can be said to represent interest income: the remainder is, in effect, repayment of capital since after one year of inflation at 5% the holder's capital has been eroded in real terms by that amount. This process is not overt since the nominal number of pounds in the building society account stays the same.

Land has characteristics which are really the opposite of a building society deposit. Real capital value has been more than maintained but the actual income yield is extremely low, historically about 2-3%. Naturally, such an asset has proved very safe over a long period, but it is unlikely to yield a sufficient regular *income*. In terms of our typical portfolio, the yield quoted below is rather optimistic since, to yield such a regular income from land holdings, blocks of land would have to be sold regularly, which would incur considerable transaction costs and the depletion of the land would of course be dangerous since it is the only asset in the portfolio with a long-term record of substantial real returns.

In order to provide a fair balance between capital maintenance, capital growth, and income, a sensible asset portfolio might therefore consist of:

30% equities
20% Gilt-edged stock
30% Building society deposits
20% land

The following are the annual average real pre-tax returns on those assets since 1946 in the case of equities, gilt-edged, and building society deposits and since 1949 in the case of land. It is assumed that all income is consumed and *not* re-invested.

Equities	+1.1% p.a.
Gilts	−1.7% p.a.
Building society	+0.65% p.a.
Land	+8.0% p.a.
Weighted average	+2.2% p.a.

Source: de Zoete and Bevan's *Gilt, Equity and Building Society Indexes, 1984,* and *'The Farmland Market'* (August, 1984).

This figure of 2.2% p.a. is a typical real long run yield on capital. At one time, indeed, this would have been a typical interest rate and if inflation were eliminated completely these are undoubtedly the sort of interest rate levels to which we would return. The average interest rate betwen 1918 and 1950 was about 3.5%.

In order to determine what amount of capital we now require to produce an income of, say £10,000 per annum over an indefinite period, we must multiply that income by 100/2.2, which is £454,545 – not far short of half a million pounds. But surely, some may object, I could place my £454,000 in a building society today and earn about 10% before tax – say £45,000 per annum. But even today, with historically very high real interest rates, about half of the £45,000 is in fact "consumed capital" – that is, a repayment of capital which has come in the form of "interest" and which therefore reduces the ability of the capital to maintain a given level of real income. Historically, as the statistics show, the real yield is only 2.2%; any amount above that will only compensate for inflation at best. If inflation were nil the "10%" building society interest rate would probably be about 2.2%. A similar process applies to all the other assets in our portfolio.

THE CAPITAL VALUE OF UNEARNED BENEFITS

Now let us return to our two couples: firstly, the unemployed man with a wife and two children. The total value of the unemployment benefit, allowances and subsidies for clothing, furniture, and housing or rent allowances (together with various discretionary benefits not usually included in the basic entitlements but undoubtedly due to such a family) is about £108 per week. A working married man with two children would have to earn £151 per week in order to earn such an income after tax and national insurance. To employ someone at that wage, an employer would have to pay a total of about £170 per week. If we apply our capital yield factor of 100/2.2 to the equivalent annual wage of £8,840 per annum, we discover that the amount of capital required to sustain the real income of our typical unemployed man and family over an indefinite period is £401,800 (see Appendix I).

Now let us consider a retired senior manager who is married. He will have been earning £25,000 per annum and will have retired on, say, 60% of his final salary. He will therefore "earn" £15,000. He will have paid off his mortgage on a house worth, say, £75,000, and he will have furniture, jewellery, and other items worth about £30,000, income from which will be used to supplement his pension, and he will own a car valued at £7,000.

96

The capital: yield factor indicates a capital equivalent of £680,000 to produce his retirement pension of £15,000 per annum. His other capital totals £142,000. Therefore, the capital required to maintain a standard of living equivalent to the retired manager over an indefinite period is £822,000 (see Appendix I).

Naturally, actuarial assessment of pension rights would indicate a lower capital requirement. However, the point here is that the possession of £822,000 will not produce an *income* higher than our retired senior manager. It must also be remembered that the senior manager's pension rights have been bought out of tax relief while the "wealthy" individual has already paid income tax in accumulating his capital.

The purchase of an annuity for both families could theoretically be cheaper but as Government itself discovered in the case of inflation proof civil servant pensions, a *real* income annuity cannot be bought.

The unemployed man's benefits are equivalent to the income of a man who owns capital of £401,000. Our retired businessman is the equivalent of a man who owns capital of £822,000. But if, instead of the *benefits* of such capital they were given the capital and told to support themselves indefinitely, they would both be termed "wealthy" and on their death would pay Capital Transfer Tax at the following rates:

Unemployed man: Capital £401,000   Tax £170,000
Retired businessman: Capital £822,000   Tax £420,000

Even on the assumption that both families split their capital evenly between man and wife, then the respective tax liabilities would be £110,000 and £360,000.

These taxes were designed to tax *wealth*. On close examination, we see that an unemployed man with a wife and children is actually wealthy and a retired senior manager has excessive wealth – enough to have more than 50% of his capital confiscated on death. It goes to the state, which has "saved" its own £822,000 capital for other purposes while the senior manager supported himself. Even on the basis of the state only supporting him at the benefit level of or unemployed man, it has saved the use of £400,000.

Either an unemployed man in our society is wealthy or the man who supports himself to the same standard of living without recourse to the state is poor. If the unemployed are considered wealthy, then the value of the benefits should be cut to that level yielded by capital on which Capital Transfer Tax is at present not payable – which would halve the existing entitlements.

Husband nil rate CTT band:		£64,000
Wife nil rate CTT band:		£64,000
Total free of CTT		£128,000
Constant real income (2.2%)		£2,816
		or £54 per week

If, on the other hand, the man who receives the income equivalent to the benefits of an unemployed man is considered *not* wealthy (which is not an unreasonable assumption!) then any family owning enough capital (£400,000) to produce that income should not pay CTT. This would mean raising the nil rate band for CTT to £200,000 for each spouse.

The ludicrous situation which has arisen is due partly to the distorting effect of inflation on capital and partly to the ever higher levels of social benefits. On grounds of logic, fairness, and family independence from the state, the present levels of capital taxation must be reduced. It is illogical for a government which believes in the virtues of family life as the principal bulwark of social stability and progress to deprive those families, who have done most to sustain *themselves*, of the capital which will help future generations to maintain their independence.

BIAS AGAINST THE LESS EDUCATED

Capital taxes are often thought to be fairer and less economically destructive than income taxes. They are assumed not to distort market signals or destroy work incentives – they are merely supposed to prevent others (usually relatives of the wealthy) enjoying privileges for which they have not worked themselves.

However, capital taxes *do* distort incentives, especially the incentive to provide for a family. They *do* distort the economy as the investments in insurance companies and agricultural land show. But most important of all capital taxes discriminate unfairly between the long established educated middle class family and the newly established less educated working class family which has only just acquired wealth through commercial success. While the wealth of the middle class family can be passed on either tangibly (with good accountants advice) or intangibly through the purchase during lifetime of a good education, books and a highly skilled environment for their children, the working lass family will be unaware of these possibilities, or may only be in a position of afford them after their children have grown up. The successful working class entrepreneur will therefore lose, through capital taxation, the advantages which others could pass on in non pecuniary form.

Capital taxes therefore are a direct discrimination against the less educated (but nevertheless equally successful) family which has taken substantial risks in order to acquire wealth (and serve their fellow citizens) but which happens to store that wealth in the form of money. It is important to emphasise in this connection that entrepreneurship and successful wealth creation is not just a question of ability and hard work on the part of the individual but also a question of statistical probability. So difficult is the establishment of a successful company that most attempts fail. In considering the very real risk of losing his present employee status, his savings and even his family home a potential entrepreneur assesses the wealth which would accrue to him *and his family* should he prove to be successful. If he assumes, as he may well do, faced with UK capital taxation, that the rewards do not balance the enormous risks he will simply not attempt to establish a business. On a national scale few individuals will attempt and even fewer will succeed in entrepreneurship and job creation.

Government always views wealth *after* it has been created. It finds it "unacceptable" and taxes it. In so doing it is destroying the prospects of general wealth creation, for it has upset the balance between risk and reward. The greater the rewards, the greater is the indication of risk. If the risk were small, there would be many competing entrepreneurs, each would be far less wealthy and consumers would get a better, more extensive and cheaper service. However, Government's high taxation of commercial rewards (in addition to income tax!) prevents other entrepreneurs entering the field and consumers are therefore not well served, although the very *few* entrepreneurs will, paradoxically, do exceptionally well. It is more comfortable for an entrepreneur to pay (even high) taxes on monopoly profits than to pay lower taxes on profits reduced by fierce competition!

As the various case studies in this book demonstrate, this is not an unusual effect of excessive Government intervention. Those they claim to represent suffer most and those they claim to be taxing suffer least. Indeed, as we see from the discussion (below) of agricultural and other reliefs from excessive capital taxation, reliefs take the form most convenient to the most wealthy and the least convenient to everyone else.

RELIEFS AND ALLOWANCES FOR CTT

Capital Transfer Tax, like most other taxes, has spawned a confusing array of special reliefs and allowances. It is a sensible aim to minimise these where they lead to investment distortions and establish clear, consistent, and generally understandable rules which equate tax rates with actual tax take and do not provide scope for loopholes and distortions – so ably exploited for commercial gain by financial institutions. In some cases, (e.g. discounted bonds) the schemes can only be implemented through insurance companies. Many such fiscal privileges accrue to institutional but not to private investment; yet our aim must be to allow a genuine undistorted choice for individuals by refusing to accept any scheme which excludes private initiative, or taxes such initiatives disproportionately.

As in all other areas of high taxation an alert family may be able to so invest their capital as to avoid paying the highest rates. Such forms of investment are rarely *economically* sensible – merely fiscally astute! In fact, since many are unaware of allowances and time-sensitive reliefs (10-year cumulation, 7-year land ownership etc it is only those few who employ professional advisers in time that take advantage of the reliefs.

Those who need to hold on to capital until death to support themselves should not be penalized by paying higher rates than those who transfer at lifetime rates. Death rates would need to be halved to equal lifetime gift rates, bringing such rates into line with average rates charged in other European countries.

PRINCIPLES FOR CAPITAL TAXATION

The continuity and independence of the family is the principal aim of any government which wishes to see the reduction in the role of the state. The ability of families to support themselves and not become a burden on the state must depend crucially on their ability to accumulate, invest, and pass on the fruits of their labour to succeeding generations. The progress of families, the health of the nation, and the emanicipation of the individual are enhanced as we graduate from feudal dependence to the increasing ownership of personal capital.

Longer retirement and less formal working mean more independence for more people who have increasing recourse to long-term support on capital rather than a contractual right to income. Both unemployment and new working patterns (including more part-time work) demand an individualized structure of support which cannot be provided by the state. The state should therefore encourage – and certainly not destroy through capital taxation – individual and family capital ownership.

Contractual income rights are as valuable as capital ownership. Those whose independently supported incomes are lower than the value of state benefits cannot be classed and taxed as 'wealthy'.

No fiscal preferences for institutions can be allowed to militate against the freedom of the individual to choose his form of investment. There must be no special agreements or "grey areas" which put institutions at an advantage over the individual.

Fiscal privileges for individuals owning land must not artificially stimulate the price of farms out of the reach of genuine farmers.

The distribution of wealth should be through the challenge of market forces, not arbitrary confiscation through taxation of capital.

CONCLUSION

Profits and wealth are subject to purely quantitative definition – there is no attempt to relate wealth to effort expended. Profits and wealth are not always measurable. When they are *not* measurable they are ignored for taxation purposes even though they constitute a large portion of individual remuneration. Company "perks", paid holidays, internal waste, relaxed working conditions, paid unemployment all constitute non monetary profits and income but they are consumed without being explicitly defined in terms of money. Others *pay* for such advantages – and out of taxed income!

Similarly when industry is so successful as to greatly reduce the cost of its products (televisions, computers etc can often fall to a tenth of their initial real price) then consumers receive a "profit" equal to the amount by which the price has fallen, but they are not taxed on that increased wealth. Indeed, since VAT and other sales taxes are related to the gross price the revenue actually loses money! Meanwhile the company which provides this increased wealth is taxed heavily even though such taxation *reduces* the chances of lower unit costs and therefore higher wealth for consumers.

The tax treatment by the British Government of those whom political prejudice has arbitrarily categorised as "wealthy" illustrates four common characteristics of Government intervention:

1. Intervention is based on ill defined states of "wealth", "poverty", "profits" etc.
2. Tax thresholds, rates and cut off points are set at a level which do not affect the wealth enjoyed by the average Cabinet Minister.
3. The entire economy suffers from the misallocation of investment which the tax causes.
4. Those who are best able to understand and keep abreast of changes in the law or tax will avoid its worst effects, passing on the main burden to the less wealthy and less informed.

The cases illustrated in this paper show that even for the most basic definitions of politics Government is not sure whether those whom they thought wealthy are poor or whether those they thought poor are wealthy. They find that very average families are heavily taxed while real wealth is relatively unscathed. The process makes land holders, insurance companies and accountants wealthy by decimating businesses which *really* add value and makes farming a privileged profession for those least interested in farming.

But perhaps the most important failure of Government and politicians is their inability to understand that *continued* wealth and profits in a *market* economy can only accrue to those who serve their fellow citizens. It is only in an economy where Government perpetuates monopolies, distorts markets and taxes excessively that wealth will signal *exploitation* rather than service of the people. For in such a society neither competitors nor free consumers can effectively challenge the wealthy. It is the communist countries and the more socialist western countries which sporn a *few* immensely rich individuals. The lack of market efficiency and entrepreneurship permits many very lucrative avenues for monopoly profits by the few. The wealthy farmer, trader or builder in the Eastern block is *covertly* encouraged by the State. He is doing a good job but to admit and advertise such wealth in a socialist State would be politically impossible. Other *potential* farmers, traders or builders remain unaware of these lucrative possibilities and are therefor prevented in effect from supplying more goods to the many and reducing the profits of the few.

There is no difference between such direct discouragement of enterprise and encouragement of monopoly profits in communist countries and the same effect achieved by higher taxes in western countries. In both cases Government intervenes to prevent information about consumer needs reaching producers, perpetuates monopoly profits by discouraging competition and stultifies commercial growth.

In such circumstances wealth *is* of course unjustified, unchallengeable and eminently taxable. But the answer is not high taxation but the removal of the causes of unjustified profits and wealth – and that means the elimination of Government subsidies and controls which *promote* the waste of resources and the concentration of wealth.

APPENDIX I

A. Unemployed man with a wife and two children – entitlements

Unemployment benefit	46.00
Child benefit	13.70
Supplementary benefit	5.05
Housing benefit (assume full rent & rates)	25.00
School meals free (two children)	5.00
Central heating subsidy (5 rooms)	4.20
Laundry costs (first 45p excluded)	Estimate 3.00
Purchase or replacement of beds, carpets, chairs, bedclothes, dining table, etc	Estimate 4.00
Internal and external decoration, repairs maintenance	Estimate 3.00

108.05

Post-tax income	108.05
Equivalent income pre tax and national insurance	151.00
Cost to employer of employing that income	170.00
Long term capital to yield real income of £8,840 p.a.	£401,818

B. Senior manager retired from £25,000 p.a. post

	Capital value
Pension (60% final salary) £15,000	£680,000
House (no mortgage)	75,000
Savings	30,000
Furniture, jewellery etc	30,000
Car	7,000
Total capital + capital equivalent	£822,000

APPENDIX II

Tax Yields CGT and CTT

Financial year	CGT (£m)	CTT (£m)
1966-67	7	–
1967-68	16	–
1968-69	47	–
1969-70	128	–
1970-71	139	–
1971-72	155	–
1972-73	208	–
1973-74	324	–
1974-75	382	–
1975-76	387	118
1976-77	323	259
1977-78	340	311
1978-79	353	323
1979-80	431	401
1980-81	508	424
1981-82	525	480
1982-83	632	499
1983-84	671	601
1984-85	710	674

On the assumption that present indexation of CGT allowances continues, HM Treasury estimates that by 1990 Capital Gains Tax yield will be a mere £250m.

5 Tax relief on Mortgage interest

Tax relief on mortgage interest payments cost the Exchequer £4,500m in the fiscal year ending 1986. In effect the Government is injecting £4,500m per annum of money demand into the housing market, or more precisely into the housing *loan* market. This Keynesian principle sits somewhat uneasily with the Government's general financial and economic policies. The subsidy is justified, often by the "driest" of Government supporters on the basis of two untenable assumptions. Firstly it is maintained that any extra injection of the nation's resources into housing demand will increase the housing stock. Secondly it is argued that the policy encourages home ownership (with other concomitant Conservative virtues!) and is of particular help to the first time buyer. Both of these claims have proved illusory.

Let us first examine the "demand creates supply" argument. The mere channelling of a subsidy to home buyers is unlikely to change the *real* demand for house ownership. What it will create is a demand for tax relief which can of course only be obtained by borrowing to fund the house purchase. More importantly such a subsidy, having no direct connection with house *construction* will not contribute to an increase in the housing stock or at least any increase is likely to be out of all proportion to the injection of Government revenue. In addition the quantity, quality, type and location of housing constructed or preserved is likely to suit the requirements of the wealthy and older members of society seeking tax shelter rather than the specific accommodation needs of home seekers. Because of the planning and construction periods involved any increased money demand for housing is as likely to lead to house builders and land owners providing the same amount of houses and land but at a higher profit.

As the table shows, the massive rise in net mortgage advances between 1968 and 1982 (out of all proportion to inflation in the same period) was accompanied both by a decline in the proportion of GDP devoted to housing capital expenditure and in the number of houses completed each year which fell from 378,000 in 1969 to 176,000 in 1982. It is interesting to note that land prices over the same period rose roughly in line with inflation so that this cost component cannot account for any of the discrepancy between advances for house purchase and the record of house construction. The massive change in net mortgage advances per completed house from 2.26 in 1969 to 77.4 in 1982 must cast serious doubt on the Government's whole housing policy. The UK spent only 2.2% of GDP on house building in 1982 compared to an OECD average of 5%, France's 5% and Germany's 6%.

A comparison of the inflation adjusted increase in advances for housing and actual increase in the housing stock between 1969 and 1982 is even more dramatic:

Increase net advances	Inflation adjusted	Increase stock of dwellings
1,587%	1,226%	+13%

The only way to increase house ownership is to increase the supply of suitable housing. If there is any excuse whatsoever for subsidy it must surely be for house building, not debt funded purchase of existing houses.

The second argument in favour of mortgage interest relief (that home ownership is increased and first time buyers benefit) assumes that an increase in house ownership is synonymous with an increase in the numbers of people owning a house. One of the major social changes over recent years is the increasing numbers of home owners who have more than one house. To the high tax payer, relief at his marginal rate of tax makes the cost of financing his principal dwelling so low that he has ample funds to invest in a second home. Sine the housing market has as its principal ingredient an attractive market in tax relief it is more than a little naive of Government to assume that those who benefit will be first time buyers who by definition are unlikely to be high tax payers (if they are they have no need of the subsidy!). Tax stimulated demand raises the price of housing above what it would otherwise be so that first time buyers must raise larger deposits as the nominal house price rises. In addition the poorer first time buyer must compete with richer first time buyers whose relief at *their* marginal rate of tax is of far more value than to his poorer "competitor". In addition the *family* first time buyer must compete with a tax subsidised *single* person whose accommodation will be under-utilised.

HOUSE OWNERSHIP AND LABOUR MOBILITY

In the United Kingdom house ownership by the under 25s is the highest of any industrial democracy.

United Kingdom	30%
Canada	17%
Australia	23%
Holland	16%
Germany	4%
France	7%

If this position had arisen out of rational choice undistorted by the activities of Government it might be a praiseworthy achievement – a signal of a highly stable and prosperous country. But nothing could be further from the truth! Young people in Britain also happen to be among the poorest, least mobile and most unemployed in any advanced industrial country. Many are seduced into house purchase and high debt by the tax subsidy, others are forced into home ownership because the private rented sector has been destroyed by Government legislation and, in effect, taxed by the subsidy to house ownership. Once having bought a house they are trapped when unemployment strikes and house prices fall. If they can sell at all the price will be so low compared to the area where there is employment that remaining unemployed may well be preferable.

Much of the very large differences in house prices between more and less prosperous regions is due in no small measure to the higher Government subsidy for housing in rich areas than in poor! For instance the richer South of England receives a larger subsidy through mortgage interest relief on large incomes than does the North of England on its smaller average incomes.

If there were no mortgage interest relief the difference between house prices would be less, the rented market would be more developed and the young would not be seduced in mistaken and inflexible investment in house ownership.

BUILDERS AND BUILDING SOCIETIES – TAX FINANCED INEFFICIENCY

If there is one certain result of a financial windfall it is that it will be wasted by the recipients. The £4,500m which the Government lavishes on those who buy house mortgages finds its way swiftly into the hands of those who provide mortgages and build houses. The Building Societies, which are erroneously described as "non profit making" take their profits in the form of higher salaries and less efficiency: We can compare 1960, when Schedule A tax counterblances mortgage interest relief, to 1983 after 21 years of a net mortgage subsidy.

Management, Expenses and Depreciation as a percentage
of mortgage amounts advanced.

1960	3.2%
1983	5.1%

(see also Appendix IV)

Considering the advances in office automation and the increased efficiency of electronic information systems this decline in efficiency is quite remarkable.

The other beneficiaries of the Governments largesse, housebuilders, have not only taken higher profits from fewer houses built but their productivity has declined radically. The builders Laing note that the same house built by their workforce in the 1930's in one month today takes 2 months while the industry average is 5 months!

Even if we examine the historical effectiveness of the mortgage interest tax relief on the increase in house ownership, it is of interet to see that the steepest rise in the proportion of dwelling owner occupied in the UK was between 1950 and 1960 when, because of the Schedule A tax on home ownership (abolished in 1962) there was no *net* financial incentive to house owners from mortgage interest relief.

Apart from the tax incentive to borrow for house purchase (whether funds are needed or not) there is also an incentive for higher rate tax payers to save with building societies since only a so called "composite rate" of 25% is deducted at source. There is therefore a cash flow advantage until the Inland Revenue claims the higher rate applicable. The savings advantage for the rich, combined with the prospect of a tax subsidised loan for all savers, has had a dramatic effect on the expansion of Building Societies. Even after adjusting for inflation the rise in the assets of all societies, especially since 1960, has been staggering:

1960	£3183m	increase 1600%
		inflation 567%
1980	£5400m	real incr. 1033%

Between 1970 and 1982 Building Societies share of personal sector savings rose from 35% to 47%. Nevertheless much of the *recent* rise in mortgage lending has come from the banks. Of the increase of £6.4 billion in net mortgage advances between 1980 and 1982 no less than 70% was due to increased lending by the commercial banks. The recent pressure on bank lending, money supply and hence inflationary pressure has come principally from the personal sector and mortgage lending in particular, helping to make the profitability of housing debt a self fulfilling prophecy!

This diversion of savings from commercial investment to housing, aided by Government, has benefited housebuilders, building societies, existing home owners and high tax payers. It has not helped those who own no house nor the expansion of the housing stock but has served to confirm the advantages of inflation by providing further incentives for debtors.

Mortgage Interest Tax Relief is a typical Government intervention. It brings about the reverse of what it intends and at considerable cost in terms of economic efficiency. Mortgage interest Relief
– seduces many into unsustainable house ownership
– costs £4,500m per annum
– distorts capital markets and causes labour immobility
– raises house prices without increasing the amount spent on house *building*
– has no demonstrable effect on home ownership
– militates against the first-time buyer
– makes monetary control more difficult
– helps to instigate and confirm the advantages of inflation
– promotes the construction of house types unsuitable for families and childlren who need them
– increases the economic differences between regions.

Even by the standards of Government intervention this is a quite staggering list of "achievements".

House Prices and Fixed Investments in Dwellings
UK 1956 – 1982

Year	New House Prices £	Investment in construction of Dwellings £m
1956	2280	634
1957	2330	615
1958	2390	582
1959	2410	646
1960	2530	721
1961	2770	791
1962	2950	856
1963	3160	956
1964	3460	1217
1965	3820	1286
1966	4100	1374
1967	4340	1525
1968	4640	1675
1969	4880	1667
1970	5180	1643
1971	5970	1898
1972	7850	2254
1973	10690	2686
1974	11340	3187
1975	12406	4149
1976	13442	4726
1977	14768	4685
1978	17685	5270
1979	22728	5862
1980	27244	6387
1981	28508	5500
1982	31678	6073

1962 was the year when the real *net* tax advantage of mortgage interest relief began.

Real annual rise in house prices 1956 – 1962 2% pa	Real annual rise in house prices 1962 – 1971 5.3% pa
Rise in house prices 1956 – 1982 X 9.6	Increase in fixed investment in construction of dwellings X 7.1

APPENDIX II

Year	Mortgage Net Advances Banks and Building Societies £m	Change over previous year	Housing Capital Exp. as % of GDP	UK Houses completed 000s	Net Advances £m per House completed
1969	858	–	5%	378	2.26
1970	1245	+45%	4.5%	362	3.44
1971	1823	+46%	4.6%	364	5.0
1972	2783	+52%	4.8%	331	8.4
1973	2831	+2%	4.3%	305	9.28
1974	2372	−16%	4.0%	280	8.47
1975	3650	+53%	4.4%	322	11.33
1976	3871	+6%	4.3%	325	11.9
1977	4266	+10%	3.93%	314	13.58
1978	5435	+21%	3.9%	289	18.8
1979	6487	+19%	3.5%	252	25.7
1980	7235	+11%	3.0%	240	30.1
1981	9470	+30%	2.4%	205	46.2
1982	13,623	+44%	2.2%	176	77.4

Sources   Housing and construction statistics
Lloyds Bank
Own calculations

APPENDIX III

First time Buyers

The number of loans to first time buyers as a percentage of all loans.

Year	% of all loans
1969	63%
1970	61%
1971	60%
1972	57%
1973	52%
1974	51%
1975	47%
1976	49%
1977	48%
1978	47%
1979	45%
1980	47%
1981	49%
1982	54%
1983	52%
1984	52%

The rise in the percentage of first time buyers after 1980 has been due largely to the Government's policy of selling council houses.

John Ermisch in a Policy Studies Institute paper "Housing Finance, Who Gains?" wrote: "The best estimate is that new purchasers now receive a subsidy on a given dwelling half as much as an existing owner would receive."

Building Societies

Management Expenses and depreciation as percentage of Advances 1960 – 1983

Year	Mortgages Amount Advanced £m	Management, Expenses & depreciation £m	Expenses as % of Advances
1960	560	18	3.2%
1961	546	20	3.6%
1962	613	22	3.5%
1963	849	25	2.9%
1964	1043	28	2.6%
1965	955	32	3.3%
1966	1245	37	2.9%
1967	1463	42	2.8%
1968	1590	49	3.1%
1969	1559	57	3.6%
1970	1954	68	3.4%
1971	2705	85	3.1%
1972	3630	102	2.8%
1973	3513	119	3.4%
1974	2945	145	4.9%
1975	4908	197	4.0%
1976	6183	237	3.8%
1977	6745	297	4.4%
1978	8808	363	4.1%
1979	9002	449	4.9%
1980	9503	590	6.2%
1981	12005	732	6.1%
1982	15033	815	5.4%
1983	19357	996	5.1%

Mortgage interest subsidy has its biggest impact in times of high inflation when interest rates are higher and therefore the subsidy greater in money terms. In addition because much of the "interest" in effect represents repayment of capital, mortgagors receive tax relief on their repayments!

It is interesting to note the 70% rise in mortgages advanced between 1962 and 1964 – the first two years of the effective *net* subsidy to mortgagors.

6 The Market Case against the Common Market (1984)

Eleven years after Britain entered the Common Market 48% of the British people think membership of the EEC a "bad thing" and only 10% think membership of the EEC has increased understanding. 70% of industrial respondents to a recent survey by the Institute of Directors said they "had seen no advantages from membership" and even 60% of British farmers could see no advantages!

The balance sheet for the United Kingdom after 11 years is indeed somewhat discouraging with UK non oil exports to the original 6 members of the Community having risen from 22% of total exports in 1973 to only 25% today – a smaller increase than in our trade with, for example, the Middle East.

Although the motivation for the original "Common Market" was undoubtedly political, the first steps were rightly seen to be economic: to agree and enforce basic rules of free trade, a gradual reduction in customs duties, the establishment of intra community economic structures and, finally, common laws and a common monetary system arising out of a common Parliament. At each step the rules were ignored or circumvented for national purposes and the aim of each stage aborted. The Community nevertheless rewarded itself for this lack of success by proceeding to the next stage! As the reality of economic and political failure became more evident, the more grandiose, and verbose were the calls for a "broader vision" – a not untypical response by collectivists in the face of their own failure!

Because the EEC is not seen as a forum for free and fair trade, even between partners, never mind internationally, much political time is spent discussing management of the EEC budget and trade balances: 1983

Country	EEC Trade Balance	Net Budget Position £m.
UK	−1140	−1122
France	−7866	−3.5
Germany	+5130	−1710
Netherlands	+7980	+217
Italy	−1710	+830
Ireland	−855	+447
Belgium/Luxembourg	+1140	−231
Denmark	+570	+192
Greece	−1539	+312

The Germans' large budget contribution can be seen as a very good investment in their access to other countries industrial markets. In addition much of the German gross contribution to the budget flows back through the CAP to German farmers whose poor competitive position in the face of French farming is protected through the adjustment of the green currenices. There are of course no such green currency adjustments for trade in the goods where French industry is at a competitive disadvantage against German industry so that less official and – as the table shows not very effective – means are used!

France, with a highly centralised Government-dominated industrial structure (impervious to consumer preferences) and lacking significant domestic energy sources has a negative trade balance with the rest of the community 7 times the size of the UK deficit. Its support for an EEC funded agricultural policy from which it benefits more than most is therefor understandable.

Out of a budget, 75% of whose disposable income goes to agriculture, UK farmers have,not surprisingly, done quite well. Between 1979 and 1983 the percentage of the CAP benefiting UK farmers doubled and in 1983 UK receipts totalled £1,000m. Naturally this largesse has encouraged our capital intensive farming industry to expand. Whereas we were, in 1973, self sufficient in only one CAP supported product we are now at least self sufficient in all:

UK self sufficiency 1982:

wheat	128%
barley	115%
sugar	145%
beef	106%
pigmeat	102%
butterfat	117%
non fat milk products	120%

It is a characterstic of Governments and non market institutions that production, sale, and self sufficiency are regarded as laudable aims. They rarely understand that by far the most important criterion is cost. There is no limit to the extent of self sufficiency we could achieve in all products if we were foolish enough to spend all our money on that irrelevant goal.

On the basis of *employment* productivity the UK has the most efficient farming industry in Europe:

Country	EEC Farm Production	% Domestic Workforce on land
UK	14	2.8
Belgium	3.5	2.9
Denmark	4.1	8.4
France	27	8.4
Italy	21	13
Luxembourg	0.1	5.6
Netherlands	8.6	4.5
Ireland	2.3	18.9
Germany	18.8	5.8
Greece	na	28
Spain	na	20
Portugal	na	32

However, since the average British farm is three times the size of the average farm in Ireland, France or Denmark and four times the average in Germany, production in relation to land and capital use may be less favourable. If market forces were allowed fuller rein in the EEC we might begin to find out which country or which farming methods were more efficient but it is a characteristic of a non market environment that no one knows whether what they are doing is worth while or not. What is certain, however, is that applying the logic of the CAP inevitably leads to grave problems even for those who, like the United Kingdom, superficially benefit so much. As EEC milk producers are now learning to their cost, self sufficiency or over-production of goods that cannot be sold will in the end burden even the most efficient farmers.

We must of course recognise that agricultural production is not comparable with industrial production: supply is not so susceptible to demand and price changes, products are not all storable, land supply is limited and a capital intensive structure is vulnerable to sudden price fluctuations. However, in continental Europe agriculture is a recognised vote buyer and the UK cannot escape the conclusion that the CAP is designed and used to preserve farmers rather than agriculture and in so doing it is more likely to destroy the latter in the name of the former! In addition the structure of the EEC is such that the rural CAP serves as an effective regional and social policy on the Continent while the industrial regional problems of the UK receive much less attention (7.6% of the 1982 EEC budget was spent on regional support). It may be one way of reducing the UK's net budget contributions if the Government were to set out to concentrate job creation schemes on agricultural projects but like so much economic pragmatism in Europe, the mere imitation and extension of illogical interventionism will not in the end benefit either the UK or the EEC.

If the CAP logic of subsidised prices, import controls, green currencies and volume controls through levies were applied to other industrial sectors it would be unacceptable, even in the EEC. If for example cars were traded at special "green currency" rates then, as the DM rose against the Pound and British cars became more competitive in Germany the politicians would intervene and reverse the situation by establishing a new artifical exchange rate to protect German car manufacturers. This was of course impossible for cars but it is in fact exactly what happened when German farmers were protected from French food exports from the early 1970's. If, to continue the analogy, the EEC bought cars into intervention stocks at price high enough to sustain the smallest and least profitable producers then the costs would be passed on to all taxpayers, directly through car prices and indirectly through general taxation. Car stocks and inefficiency would grow and eventually, because the political lobby of, say, BL and Fiat producers could resist price cuts then a levy on all car production would be imposed. This would prevent Jaguar, Mercedes and BMW from producing their successful cars as well as preventing BL and Fiat from producing their less successful cars. Had no other regime than the one described above ever been known for the car industry then such protectionism would be taken for granted. In fact of course there was no protection fo the German car market as the DM rose in value but German car producers competed successfully and remain the most successful car manufacturers in Europe.

In addition to the many illegal subsidies, customs restrictions and failure to follow community policy, perhaps the most damaging activities of the EEC are in its external relations with trading partners.

The EEC "manages" much of UK trade through export and import agreements with non EEC countries. 40% of Japanese trade with the EEC is covered by Community negotiated "voluntary export restraints". These prevent free trade, guarantee European producers a market they do not deserve, raise prices in the EEC and provide the Japanese with an effective subsidy. For cars alone the UK subsidy to the Japanese was estimated to be £260m per annum. The subsidy arises because, by restricting the number of Japanese cars below the number British people wish to buy, the Japanese car maker can raise his price. He therefore makes a bigger profit on each car than if the market were not so restricted.

One-third of EEC aid to the Third World is in the form of food which tends to compound developing country problems by depressing local prices, preventing indigenous development and increasing their import dependence. The community's "STABEX" (Stabilisation of export earnings) scheme compensated developing countries for fluctuations in their export earnings from basic commodities on which they were particularly dependent. This merely encouraged their dependence, making their economies even more vulnerable and badly diversified – a typical example of tackling *symptoms* and postponing the removal of *causes*.

EEC enlargement to 12 member states provides a very great threat not only to the budget but to developing countries. The CAP will stimulate EEC domestic production from Greece, Spain and Portugal of many of the products on which developing countries rely for foreign exchange earnings.

EEC imports from developing countries compared to production in Greece Spain and Portugal

Commodity	EEC (9) % from LDC's	% from Gr, Sp + Port.
Fresh vegetables	62	16
Fresh fruit	50	26
Olive oil	54	31
Prepared vegetables	35	33
Prepared fruit	39	19
Wine	10	71

There are few political questions which today can unite South America, USA, developing countries, Australia and New Zealand, but the activities of the EEC in the world food trade is certainly one of them. The degree of subsidy and "trade management" externally is mirrored internally by the lack of an effective freely competitive market. It is that area of activity to which the EEC devotes 75% of its disposable budget, which the USA has always regarded as a major generator of industrial growth and in which both sides of the Atlantic see a source of electoral support – agriculture – where the seeds of a serious world trade conflict are being sown. The world market in food exhibits all the characteristics of politicised intervention, artificial prices, geographic distortion resulting from artificial pricing signals and gross mismatch of suppliers and consumers. If the internal markets of the developed world cannot develop rational agricultural policies, the international situation can only deteriorate.

Although few EEC members would consider *active* extension of CAP logic to other industrial areas, Mrs Thatcher's "liberal Conservatives" have reason to fear further corporatist and interventionist activities by European institutions.

A recent report of the Energy Committee of the European Parliament on the European Gas Industry had all the interventionist and paternalist ingredients which are anathema to present UK industrial policy but which seem to typify the EEC's approach to economic questions: the Brussels Commission is urged to "examine what measures it should take and what new powers it should assume" in order to bring "more order" to the European gas market. Brussels could "approve supply contracts, set criteria for stock management, plan distribution systems, lay down rules for methods of fixing prices and tariffs" and "encourage investment". Like any other market, "order" is achieved primarily by rational suppliers and consumers competing without artificial subsidy or rigid public sector controls. Of these ingredients there is little sign.

When the European Community seeks to organise the restructuring of industries in crisis, like steel or textiles they utilise the same Government support and trade protectionism which caused the original crisis. We are now told of a crisis not in a declining sector but in a growth sector – electronics! Yet European Governments have influenced the development of that sector more than any other through the public ownership and subsidy of telecommunications, the market dominance of Government defence procurement and the protection of domestic suppliers. The United Kingdom has every reason to fear European corporatism – even more than it should fear unfair budget contributions.

Having spent many painful years breaking down corporatist interventionist logic within the UK and establishing competitive industries fit for free trade the British Government cannot afford to allow EEC trade management and protectionism to frustrate British companies profitability. Free trade in airlines, banking, insurance, agriculture and electronics would be most advantageous to the UK's earnings in Europe. It must also be in the interests of Britain's EEC partners if we could allow a positive trade balance to counteract our budget burden rather than to allow the latter to be a perpetual bone of contention.

The problem of Britain's contribution to the EEC budget cannot be solved by transferring this corporatist and protectionist logic to other areas, even if the UK may seem thereby to benefit in the short run.

The British Government should use its present position of power not just to change the system of budgetary contributions or even the distribution of EEC spending but to demand immediate progress on establishing in the EEC the same market principles of fair competition under the rule of law which it advocates at home. By recalling the original aims of the Community Mrs Thatcher can easily avoid accusations of pure nationalism and help to resolve the many conflicts within the EEC which would exist, probably in a more extreme form, if the United Kingdom were no longer a member.

CONCLUSION

One of the first acts of the European Parliament was to establish facilities for lobbying by the various national and industrial interest groups. Whereas most Parliaments only relapse into institutionalised horse-trading by non elected lobbyists after some attempt has been made to represent electors, the European Parliament was not so tardy. After all, the very institution of the European Community and its protectionist stance towards the outside world is based not on the uncomfortable demands of a democratic market but on the rather more comfortable conventions of political power. The spontaneously expressed choices of responsible individuals were never regarded with such favour as the politicised decisions of corporatist coteries.

All that was remote, inefficient and undemocratic in national government was raised to a more exalted and less accessible plain in Brussels, Strasbourg and Luxemburg. Political decisions reduce the value of economic responsibility: corporatism alienates public choice: international decisions are less accountable to an identifiable electorate. The very size of inter governmental institutions takes on a momentum which no individual can even comprehend, never mind control. Bureaucratic administration soon drives out enterprise and, in Shakespeares words "the native hue of resolution is sicklied o'er with the pale cast of thought".

The European Common Market has all these attributes in excess. It is not common, nor European nor a market. It may be the apotheosis of Government but it represents the nadir of democracy.

7 Overseas Aid by Foreign Trade (1984)

The Brandt Commission has given spurious legitimacy to those with guilty consciences about the West's "betrayal" of the "Third World" who wish to "co-ordinate", "organise" and "control markets" in the name of international compassion.

Although aid in the form of food, medicine and clothing are the basic requirements for a disaster area, and agricultural schemes can help to settle the nomadic and feed more mouths, such measures are short-term, superficial and fail to tackle root causes. The key to Third World development is an understanding of the motivations and mechanisms of international trade and of how the constraint of trade threatens even the industrialised West, which in previous centuries built its wealth on the principles it now disclaims.

If an over-populated country with no natural resources or agricultural wealth is a poor country, then Hong Kong and Taiwan are enigmas. If a country with immense natural resources and fertile land is rich, then why are Uganda and Zambia so poor? So many suffer in countries overflowing with oil and gas like Nigeria and Iran. The rich are not rich because they have been the recipients of aid or the objects of Western "co-ordination". The poor are not poor because they have received nothing. The reasons for economic success or failure are very often religious or cultural, yet there can be little doubt about the ways in which we in the industrialised countries have consciously or unconsciously prevented the developing world from realising its true potential.

Since the Second World War the Western industrialised nations have satisfied the demands of the consumer-voters by printing more money as expectations rose faster than production. Payment for the essential raw materials (by which developing countries earned their meagre foreign exchange) was made in depreciating currencies, and the materials squandered in our inefficient factories. Western trade unions and weak management caused manufactured goods prices to the developing countries to rise out of proportion to those countries' earnings from their exports to us. It was and continues to be colonialism veiled by the web of inflation and devalued money promises. Throughout the 1950s and 1960s raw material prices failed to keep pace with western inflation. In 1959 and again in 1960 the oil companies even imposed cuts in oil prices on the producer countries. OPEC was formed in September 1960 – several years after the inward-looking Common Market.

OPEC saw the world's richest countries consuming their only valuable natural resource at knock-down prices. Even today after the 1973 and 1979 oil price shocks, the typical North American pays far below market price for petrol. Between 1972 and 1979 OECD real energy prices rose by a mere 3% per annum. In neither 1973 nor 1979-80, when oil prices quadrupled and tripled respectively, did the total supply change. It was profligate Western demand, lurching from one peak of economic output to another, which raised oil prices.

As the Western economies failed to tackle basic internal distortions, preferring to procrastinate, print money, appease trade unions and pour vital world resources down the plug-hole of British Leyland and Chrysler, so world commodity markets went from boom to bust. Industrialised countries banded together in insular "common markets", keeping out Third World textiles and manufacturers and over-producing commodities which the developing world could produce more cheaply as earners of vital foreign exchange. To cover yawning trade deficits Western countries subsidised their goods into export markets, crowding out developing countries.

Britain's contribution to the Third World countries was to turn our backs on them as trade partners and join the Common Market, to which our exports have risen from 29% of the total to 43% since 1971 while our exports to developing countries with no oil resources have fallen from 17.7% to 12.4% of the total. While we have raised our imports from the EEC from 29 to 41%, we now take only 11% of our imports from developing countries without oil instead of 14% in 1971. Japanese and American investment flowing into the UK (the only tangible advantage of membership of the EEC) would dry up if we put ourselves outside protectionist walls from within which the European dispenses limited trade privileges to the poor nations.

Where we seek to control, organise and co-ordinate, we have done most harm to the Third World. If we had to recall those most responsible for the conciliation of consumer-voters, the printing of money, the toleration of economic incompetence, the subsidised consumption of raw materials and the formation of protectionist "common markets", we would be hard pressed to avoid the names of the members of the Brandt Commission.

8 A Safer Road for "young nation" debtors

We saw in Part I how the irresponsible monetary policies of developed nations stimulated an inflationary and unstable demand for oil and other commodities. Although oil was particularly prone to the control of a cartel and the price fluctuations were therefore particularly erratic, most raw materials produced by developing countries received the benefit of the "North's" money printing.

Within the industrial countries the relationship between Government as the "protector"(!) of the currency and the commercial banks (regulated by Government) who trade in money was central to the process of inflation. As the initial conduit through which Government directs inflation, the commercial banks profited from the expansion of their trade in deposits and loans. Later, as inflation began to take hold those with money tend to withdraw from long term fixed interest securities (Government bonds, corporate loan stock) and put their funds in shorter term floating rate deposits – the speciality of the commercial banks! When industry, with declining real profitability, could not finance itself in the capital markets they had increasing recourse to short term finance – from the commercial banks! Internationally the inflationary booms in commodities led commodity producers to finance their new found wealth. Being reluctant to sacrifice any equity by encouraging foreign direct investment they therefore borrowed – from the commercial banks in the developed countries. This lending to countries seemed safer than financing domestic industry, not least because the borrowers were politicians with access to taxpayers' money and inexperienced in negotiating large financial packages. Much of this highly profitable lending was inept. The value put on a country's economy (and hence its ability to service and eventually repay debt) was often based on the inflated value of only one major export commodity. As we have seen the deposits on-lent to these "sovereign" borrowers were themselves the very fabric of the inflation which had stimulated the (paper) value of the resources to which the Banks looked for implicit security!

When Governments then applied stricter monetary policies

to bring down inflation there was, paradoxically, yet another boost to commercial bank profitability – higher interest rates! The Clearing Banks in particular had a large block of "free deposits" in the sense that current accounts pay no interest. They were able to on-lend these free deposits at interest rates of up to 20% – a considerable windfall (eventually taxed in the UK in 1981). In the long run, however, Banks have been forced through competitive pressures to pay interest on current accounts and so the windfall has been largely eliminated.

Whether this process of increasing bank debt was a function of inflation, Government debt, corporate failure or international trade imbalances, the important feature is what I term the *alienation of capital* from its owners and the resulting alienation of the investor from his investment.

When an investor invests in equities or debt instruments in the capital markets he makes a deliberate personal choice of a specific company or institution with full knowledge and responsibility for the consequences. However, when a company fails to generate internal funds from profits or when a Government, because of its reputation for inflation is unable to raise debt finance in the capital markets at reasonable rates of interest the commercial banks are increasingly called upon to be an impersonal intermediary between the depositors (who did not intend to invest in companies or Government) and the debtors. It is therefore the banks (who are not qualified *investors* but the providers of short term finance) who alienate the investor from the investee and the owner from his capital.

It is particularly ironic that while the alienation of capital arises principally through bank debt, the UK Government has financed, through its Business Expansion Scheme, a system which even manages to alienate *equity* investment. The tax subsidy, designed originally to encourage *individuals* to invest *directly* in *new* companies sporned many City based *funds* investing other people's money in *established* companies.

Financial alienation is in fact a reflection of alienation in the "real" economy when companies become divorced from their consumers. If there is no market responsibility to free consumers for products and services, eventually there are no responsible markets for capital.

The expanding and increasingly profitable role of the banks in domestic and international finance established throughout the 1970's is not easily reversed. In international finance the readjustment to a more healthy regime of less bank "intermediation" and more direct investment is made more difficult by the large monolithic supranational debt agencies such as the IMF and the World Bank. They were established by Governments and, unlike private sector financial institutions, have no need to justify themselves commercially. They have acquired sufficient political power to prevent their liquidation. The following ideas therefore are an attempt to redirect their activities into less harmful pursuits.

The United Kingdom has recognised that the expansion of debt finance and particularly Bank debt is both a function and result of inflation. It has also recognised the dangers of allowing institutions to continue on a path typical of an inflationary era but one which is incompatible with a period of tight monetary control. The Government has taken various measures to reduce the role of the Banking system as the prime financial intermediary for industry and Government (tax relief on corporate bond issues, bank deposit interest taxed at source, windfall profits tax, reduction in capital allowance) and taken other measures to promote equity investment (reduction in stamp duty, BES funds, capital gains indexation). This paper recommends a parallel approach to the problems of international debt and our relations with developing countries. Such relations are dominated by Government-sponsored supranational organisations often slow to perceive and to adapt to changing trade and financial patterns.

Within the developing countries there are two basic problems, both of which have been exacerbated by actions of the industrial nations.

First there is the size and serviceability of international debt incurred by relatively rich developing countries and the shift in the relationship between direct investment or aid and the debt finance of developing countries (see Table I). The industrial countries' pursuit of tighter monetary policy transformed low interest rates into very high rates within a short period while a more economic use of basic commodities in industrial countries prevented a recurrence of the traditional 1970's "boom" in foreign exchange earnings for developing country economies. The resultant liquidity crisis exposed the inherent instability of "over-geared" economies and today the Western banking system is under some threat as a result.

It is a natural characteristic of young and growing businesses or national economies that debt finance is high in relation to equity and retained earnings; because growth is rapid and because owners naturally resist loss of control. However throughout the 1970s, corporate and sovereign borrowers were misled by very low or negative real interest rates and lenders were misled by inflated primary product prices and explicit or implicit Government guarantees. Both borrowers and lenders therefore allowed debt levels to rise out of all proportion to equity.

Second, for all debtors, whether rich or poor the ready availability of debt finance – implicitly "secured" on reserves of oil or other strategic minerals (backed by various ill-conceived EEC and IMF schemes to "stabilise export earnings") actively discouraged the natural and healthy process of LDC diversification from dependence on one or few foreign exchange earning commodities (see Table I). Today, ten of the twenty largest debtors rely for foreign exchange earnings on one commodity.

Paradoxicaly for the poorer countries whose meagre resources never allowed the luxury of the rich man's "debt crisis" there was a continuing incentive to progress from primary to manufacturing production and as a result,the poorer LDCs have experienced a far more consistent growth pattern – aided by increasing direct investment (see Tables II and III).

In all developing countres the capital, equipment and human skills required for a well balanced development are often imported by foreign investors. Grant Reuber in a study of Capital Investment in Developing Countries (Oxford 1973) found that "the higher the degree of foreign ownership the more competitive, by international standards are the production costs of the affiliate". These investors however are faced with non commercial, largely political risks – nationalization, punitive taxation, remittance controls – which they cannot control and the probability of which their purely commercial skills cannot prepare them to judge.

EXISTING RISK COVER

Industrial countries provide political risk cover principally for debt finance of exports to developing countries (and others) through such agencies as ECGD, Coface, Hermes or Exim with very little cover offered for direct investment. In the United Kingdom political risk cover for direct investment accounts for less than 1% of the liabilities under export credit guarantees. Of the seven major supranational Government sponsored organisations financing less developed countries, only two provide equity funds – CDC and IFC and in both cases equity accounts for less than 20% of total commitments.

The value to developing countries of political risk guarantees for exports from the industrial countries is somewhat doubtful. Indeed Government guarantees and covert subsidies for exports are a source of considerable Exchequer cost and international controversy among industrial countries. As far as developing economies are concerned, those subsidies and guarantees are predominantly for manufacturing exports which further retard LDC progress towards diversification of production and exports. An agreed and balanced reduction of such support in return for increased investment insurance would help to remove many causes of controversy and trade distortions between "North" and "South".

The United States and United Kingdom Governments are right to see the present high interest rates in both real and nominal terms as a necessary ingredient in the transition from an inflationary environment which promotes industrial inefficiency and primary product booms to a more stable industrial growth based on change from secondary to tertiary production in the "North" and from primary to diversified and secondary production in the "South". The failure to do this in the past has been compounded by debt finance secured on overt assets, already discovered and yielding a tangible cash flow rather than by flexible equity investment based on new ideas and future potential. Debt availability tends to perpetuate specialisations where margins are stable but are in decline while equity tends to look to diversification where margins are larger and likely to grow. Lack of such diversification in developing countries plus the violent changes in growth in industrial countries exaggerates what I term the "Yoyo" effect (see Table IV) whereby a given change in industrial countries' GDP is magnified in the corresponding change in LDC export growth.

SPECIFIC PROPOSALS FOR DIRECT INVESTMENT INSURANCE

In order to reverse activities more suited to a period of inflation and high debt the following steps will provide a new emphasis on stable real growth and direct investment in diversification in developing countries.

1. The UK Government should seek agreement from the major export credit agencies in the USA, Japan and Europe to shift 20% of political risk guarantees for debt finance to direct investment insurance. This could be done gradually over a period of years.
2. The insurance would only apply to investment in developing countries.
3. No project or company in an LDC would qualify if the activity represented more than 25% of that country's foreign exchange earnings. This would aid both primary commodity diversificatin and moves from primary to manufacturing and service activities.
4. There would be a limit to the proportion of new annual insurance which could be taken up by any one corporation.
5. The limit for investment insurance for each country would be set in relation to their need and ability to diversify their economies.
6. Political risk insurance would be available only for additional equity finance in existing projects and companies or for completely new projects and companies.
7. Existing political risk cover provided by national Governments, together with new insurance could eventually be administered by a supranational agency – possibly the World Bank (see that organisation's ideas for a Multilateral Investment Insurance Agency). The higher risk of investment insurance would be reduced if the insurer is supranational. In the face of an international organisation responsible for other forms of aid, arbitrary expropriation and remittance controls would be less likely. In addition such an organisation would be better able to co-ordinate and discipline industrial countries' export subsidies.
8. The political risk insurance would not insure against commercial failure or a collapse in commodity prices. There would be indemnity against:
    1.Nationalisation or forced sale without full market value.
    2.Dividend remittance control.
    3.Punitive taxation or duties.
    Reasonable parameters for 2. or 3. would be stipulated in the original agreement concluded by a recipient country, the investor and the agency. The terms could also include a formula for disinvestment.

We have already seen the effects of the debt crisis on the

Western banking system and the effects on "North-South" trade as overgeared LDCs try to balance high debt servicing costs with foreign exchange earnings. Not only agricultural products but increasingly cars, steel and ships are being heavily subsidised into American and European markets by major debtors. Such a process exacerbates the social and economic cost to the "North" of what would otherwise have been a more orderly consequence of free trade.

CONCLUSION

The World Bank and IMF proposal for a "Multilateral Investment Insurance Agency" does at least identify a real problem but it is a typical response from Government sponsored agencies to crises largely of their own making – further political institutions are created to counteract the effects of existing intervention. The original institutions and interventions failed not through bad intentions but because they did no more than adjust the short term signals of change (thus retarding necessary change) rather than tackle the long run causes.

This is perhaps not surprising since an honest examination of those causes would have identified as culprits those now seeking political praise for attacking symptoms!

World Bank proposals for insuring international direct investment differ from the proposals in this paper in the following ways:

MIIA
No specification of investment type.
An addition to existing schemes.
No attempt to control export credit insurance.
Larger amounts, especially for investment consortia.
No maximum project value.
Any host country for investment.
Allocation according to sponsorship.

AUTHOR'S SCHEME
Strictly diversification projects.
Changing the emphasis of existing schemes.
Shift of insurance from export credit to direct investment.

132

Larger number of smaller projects.
Limit to project amount.
Only developing countries.
Automatic allocation according to development and
diversification criteria.

Table 1

Top Ten International Debtors

Country	1983 Debt service as % of export earnings	LDC classification	% of exports in primary products fuels, metal, mineral
Brazil	115	Upper Middle Income	50
Mexico	127	Upper Middle Income	61
Argentina	132	Upper Middle Income	71
Venezuela	78	Upper Middle Income	98
Indonesia	17	Lower Middle Income	98
Phillipines	79	Lower Middle Income	71
Chile	80	Upper Middle Income	80
Turkey	20	Upper Middle Income	81
Algeria	29	Upper Middle Income	100
Malaysia	8	Upper Middle Income	81

Source: World Development Report

Aid, Direct Investment and LDC Debt Servicing

Year	Aid + Direct Investment as a % of total debt	Debt servicing % of GNP	% of exports
1970	10	1.8	13.5
1978	7.8	3.2	15.4
1979	8.4	3.5	15
1980	8.6	3.4	13.6
1981	7.9	4.1	16.3
1982	5.2	4.7	20.7

Table II

Changes in Direct Investment

	1976	1977	1978	Dollars Billion 1979	1980	1981	1982
Oil Exporting Countries	−2.5	1.8	2.3	−3.9	−0.4	1.9	−1.0
Oil Importing Countries	4.2	4.7	5.6	7.7	8.2	12.2	10.7

Source: IMF Balance of Payments Statistics Vol 34.

Table III

Most consistent growth in low income countries (non oil)

Annual % growth	1960-73	1973-79	1980-82
Low income	4.5	5.1	4.4
Middle income oil exporters	7.0	4.8	0.7
High income oil exporters	10.7	7.5	−2.0
Industrial countries	5.0	2.8	0.7

Source: IMF Survey

Table IV

Relationship between Developed Countries' GDP Growth and Developing Countries' Export Growth – the "Yoyo effect"

| Year | % change in growth | | |
	1. GDP Developed Countries	2. LDCs' Exports	Factor 2:1
1966-67	−2½	−5	2
1967-69	+2½	+4	1.6
1969-71	−2	−5½	2.7
1971-73	+2	+11	5.5
1973-75	−7	−16	2.4
1975-76	+5½	+8½	1.5
1976-78	−1	−7	4.7
1978-81	−4½	−6½	1.4

Source: World Development Report (figures taken from graph)

PART III

Government Exploits the People

It is a great irony that no commercial organisation could so
grievously and persistently exploit the people as do the agencies
of the State. Within the private sector of the economy there is a
healthy division of powers between shareholders seeking a
commercial return on their investment, management paid by
shareholders, unions who bargain for wages and competing
corporations ready to offer alternative services and prices to
free consumers and alternative conditions to wage earners.
Government provides a further check on unfair trading and
environmental pollution, and as such is merely one of many
responsible interacting agents, none of whom have any inordi-
nate power to dictate economic or social behaviour to the
others. But when Government is increasingly used by the politicians and interest groups to gain a level of power over their
fellow citizens which the *offer* of their services would never
yield them, then the absolute power of Government and the
institutions it supports become a self-justifying establishment.
Not for them the responsibility of making a return on investment or the service of consumers, not for them the burden of
proper qualifications or the encumbrance of relevant
knowledge! For them political whim and idealogical cliché are
sufficient justification, the votes of their collectivist coterie sufficient profit and control over their fellow citizens an enticing
prospect.

In the so called "public sector" there are potentially no more
problems, disasters or commercial failures than in the private
sector, the difference lies in the extent to which
1. Those failures are discernable by producers and consumers
2. They are avoidable by consumers
Where the State has the power to supress competition, disguise
costs, subsidise returns and tax captive consumers the very

signals of failure (low sales, high losses) are unavailable to producers who, even if they had a commercial incentive to act, are unable to identify never mind rectify those failures. Consumers, although grotesquely exploited and frustrated, pay for goods they do not consume and are unable to take their custom elsewhere. Personal abuse and even physical attack are not uncommon when the people are confronted with the intransigence of "public service". Devoid of the most rational, peaceful and, for producers, the most efficient signal of failure to serve – no payment – there is very little left for consumers to do!

The following brief cases of Government exploitation of the people are divided into 3 categories: "Taxploitation", the Failure of Public Enterprise and the Failure of Public Goods. It is particularly ironic that the State has been at its most exploitive and incompetent in the very area – the provision of public goods – where even the most market oriented economist would recognise some role for the Government.

1 "Taxploitation"

I have coined the term "taxploitation" to describe the process whereby, because of Government action – or deliberate inaction – a windfall or excess profit accrues to a producer and Government joins in the exploitation of the consumer by maintaining the circumstances which provide the excess profit and then taxing it. Naturally if the Government and the people had the same interests, as Democracy implies, this would not happen. It would be unthinkable for the people to exploit and tax the people! But unfortunately we know this to be far from unthinkable and Government and its well paid acolytes prefer a permanently taxed excess profit to bolster their "indispensable" functions.

Government brings about excess profits through restrictive licencing (of for instance mineral rights or television channels) through setting up or permitting cartels and monopolies (Gas, Electricity, Clearing Banking) or through import controls (for e.g. cars or television sets). All these measures restrict the amount of goods sold and hence raise their price and the profits of the producers. Where the State is the owner of the Industry the excess profit need not even be taxed, it accrues directly to the state. In the case of import controls much of the excess profit accrues to foreign producers but if, as in the case of cars, Government owns the major domestic manufacturer, an excess profit accrues to the public purse (or rather in this case a reduced loss!)

Not all "taxploitation" need involve overt pecuniary advantage, indeed most profits in protected industries and monopolies are consumed within the system in the form of waste, excess wages, poor products and incompetence, (see the case of Building Societies in Part II above). Like much else controlled by collectivists such excess profits are not overt and tangible, and so cannot attract public attention.

Perhaps the most extreme case of Government exploitation is the revenue from taxes and duties on tobacco. There is irrefutable and overwhelming evidence that tobacco use leads to some 100,000 deaths a year. Despite apparent controls on advertising, commercial and sporting sponsorship makes cigarette advertising the most prolific and all pervading of product promotions. Government could undoubtedly prevent this but chooses not to do so. The United Kingdom Government's devotion to a healthy populace is more than a little qualified by the prospect of losing £4,500m per annum in revenue from tobacco! Taxes are not raised on products to *prevent* their consumption but rather to preserve the source of the tax!

A similar process occurs when Government is the principal or only purchaser of goods and services, as for instance in health products (NHS) or armaments (Ministry of Defence). The fact that Government is spending tax payers money somewhat blunts its interests in parsimony. If poor purchasing procedures lead to excess profits for pharmaceutical companies and arms suppliers then Government *may* recoup through taxes (the large payments in each direction proving what an important function Government is!) or, more probably, those companies will grow fat and increasingly uncommercial. The only sign of this growing failure will be in their inability to obtain orders abroad although here too they will look to Government for export guarantees and subsidies "in the national interest". This kind of subsidy is, ironically, even more prodigious for arms supplies – such sales being excluded from the minimum "consensus" interest rates applicable to export loans for other commodities!

2   The Failure of Public Enterprise

It is difficult to know where to begin to chronicle the failure of "public" ownership of and subsidy for Industry. Three tragic misunderstandings underlie the philosophy of Government ownership.

1. The mistaken belief that Government ownership means public control.
2. That that which the market rejects can be sustained by Government (other than at the cost of those they are trying to help).
3. That the commercial knowledge and ability available to the people in the market place will be available to Government when it "controls" the market.

The public never have less control over industry than when the Government owns and controls industry. If Government protects a loss maker it directly contradicts the will of the people by sustaining those who failed to serve the people. When Government controls assets it controls the market so that the responsible environment which excites, motivates and creates good industrial and marketing managers is destroyed. Those able workers therefore move on, leaving the less able in the hands of political careerists and Government Ministers.

Let us look first at two industries collectivised and nationalised largely for defensive reasons – cars and shipbuilding.

A. *British Leyland* was a politically inspired accumulation of various previously successful vehicle manufacturers linked to a volume car manufacturer – Austin Morris which was in serious decline. Largely the product of the 1960's "Industrial Reorganisation Corporation" Austin Morris acquired Leyland, Jaguar, Triumph, Rover and much else which, left to their own commercial responsibility in a market uncontrolled by Trade Unions and Government, might have prospered. Instead the entire unwieldy edifice was constructed and maintained in its blissful unawareness of customer needs not only up to bankruptcy in 1974 but even today after 11 years of Government protectionism and the injection of £2,500m. Needless to say the company still cannot produce a return on capital invested. It is now teamed with the Japanese company Honda which is benefitting from British taxpayer largesse to establish itself as a potent force in car manufacturing – with or without BL! The Japanese and other foreign car makers benefitted even more from the protection by the Government of the British car market where, as a result, car prices are the highest in the world. Excess profits of hundreds of millions of pounds a year flow from the United Kingdom to Japan, Germany, France and other exporters to our Market.

It is difficult to conceive of a more disastrous Government intervention than in the United Kingdom car market. It wasn't as if cars were not in demand – no such "Keynesian" excuse could be found. But Governments do not need an excuse, no more than they need to be responsible to shareholders or customers – such embarassments are for the private sector!

B. British Shipbuilders could at least use the dramatic drop in demand for ship construction as an excuse for Government Intervention. Between 1973 and 1983 world wide ship completions fell from 30.4m tons to 15.7m tons. Even Japan lost over 50% of production over this period. British shipbuilders, like BL, was an agglomeration of many private companies, some successful, many not. Unlike BL, most relied heavily on *Government purchase* of warships rather than commercial purchase of merchant vessels. In addition ship purchase and export is one of the most artificially subsidised areas of industry in the world – special terms for finance, export credit subsidies, all the usual corporatist organisation of "incentives" to promote the inefficient and, in effect, punish the efficient and responsible.

The 1977 order for 24 ships for Poland was a classic of its kind. The order was worth £115m for British Shipbuilders. The purchaser was not the Polish Government as such but a joint venture between the British and the Polish Governments which would then charter the vessels to Poland!. Not only were the British to build the ships, subsidise their price, and lend the Poles the money to buy them on highly favourable terms, but we were also to share 50% of the risk of owning the vessels in a falling market! £28m in subsidy was available through a special "intervention fund", a further £10m subsidy through a "favourable exchange rate" plus the usual export credit support (70% ECGD guaranteed). The vessels were sold to a country in need of foreign exchange which then set them to work at charter rates low enough to undercut British owned shipping operating in the same market!!

144

Despite the undoubted crisis in world shipping, the British shipbuilding industry had, during the 1970's, a unique opportunity to diversify into offshore activities – oil production and exploration rigs, support vessels etc. They failed. After all, when a Government subsidises your activities to cover more than 50% of the purchase price of your product with no commercial shareholders demanding a reasonable return on investments who needs to go to the trouble of breaking into new markets?

C. The DeLorean car adventure is perhaps the most grotesque example of public sector "enterprise". With the possible exception of Mafia profits from the EEC's farming policy, never have so few obtained so much from so many for so little.

Mr. Delorean was a salesman, a persuasive former American motor industry executive with "high level connections". He hawked his sportscar "opportunity" around the world looking for public funds with which to indulge his fantasy. He rightly assumed that whereas any bank, investment fund or stockbroker would send him away with a flea in his ear there were so many "compassionate" Governments in the world manned by big hearted men of the people who took a less embarrassingly detailed view of his plans. Costa Rica, Spain, Portugal and others were considered but none were so forthcoming as the British Labour Government.

A more embarrassing tale of deception, misappropriation of moneys and commercial unaccountability is difficult to imagine. The British Government lost about £90m but even more important some 350 separate suppliers were owed a total of £41m when the company was liquidated. This was always the most disastrous and yet least publicised effect of Government intervention in an otherwise commercially responsible environment. Lack of accountability (who after all *is* the "Government"?) and the sudden volume and momentum of commercial activity as public money is forced into an industry, seduce suppliers into high stock levels, to rapid growth and excessive expectations. Goverment backing is a powerful force for credibility and few ask whether management can actually cope or whether the product will sell. When the end comes many long standing businesses collapse with all the loss of livelihood, life savings, house and employment which that entails. It is a typical fallacy among politicians with public money to spend that there "is nothing to lose". But this is sadly not the case. Many companies which exsisted before the "creative" intervention are permanently lost after it fails. Government money not only failed to create anything it actually destroyed what was already there!

Successful businesses do not arise overnight by mixing Government money with a car salesman. They are established by entrepreneurs and managed by businessmen who learn slowly from their mistakes and build surely on their success. Finance comes not from taxpayers but from commercial investors, banks and satisfied customers. The blending of technical, design and marketing skills is achieved through responsible management not the irresponsible whims of politicians.

3   The Failure to provide Public Goods.

If Government has a role it is to perform those tasks which, because of the characteristics of provision or consumption, cannot be adequately performed by the people. The following examples of Government incompetence fall into the category of "public good". It is indeed remarkable that Government which considers itself competent to run steel, coal, electricity, railways, postal services, nuclear power and many other industries should be such a failure when it comes to performing those minimal tasks which constitute its raison d'etre!

Even the most libertarian market economist would accept that Government should provide defence of the country but . . .

A. Defence – the case of Nimrod. The most important aspect of defence is to know when you are being attacked and one of the most important tools in the defence of Britain is the early warning aircraft – the Nimrod. In 1977 the British Labour Government ordered Nimrods from British Aerospace (State owned) and GEC Avionics – against the advice of the Government's own experts who recommended buying American "Awacs". In 1985 an official study concluded that Nimrod would enter service in 1988, five years late and at a cost of at least £1.5 billion, five times the original estimate. The Nimrod airframe was based on a 1948 Comet which uses a type of hydraulic fluid not stocked at any airfield. The alternative aircraft, the American AWAC, would now cost over £1,000m. A combination of penny pinching, poor Government purchasing and corporatist lobbying has wasted time and money and exposed the country to unnecessary risk – Quis custodiet ipsos custodes?

B. Pollution Control. In 1975 the EEC laid down the first standard for measuring the cleanliness of sea water and bathing beaches. Member States were given 10 years to bring designated beaches up to standard. Britain's list should have included some 600 beaches but the Labour Government of the day, aware of the probable cost of achieving the standards, designated only 27 beaches – even excluding such well frequented resorts as Blackpool, Brighton and Eastbourne.

Even Luxembourg, with no coastline found 39 inland beaches! Italy designated 3308 and France 1498 beaches. Even 10 years later the British Government has had to ask for more time to bring 3 of the 27 beaches up to standard.

Similar international standards of pollution control – relating to lead in petrol and sulphur emissions from power stations – have also been systematically ignored by the British Government.

C. Public Education – the Comprehensive. Few public goods are as important as decent educational standards and Government has claimed draconian and almost universal powers to impose its own view of those standards. Nothing epitomised the arrogance of the "Nanny State" more than the imposition of the comprehensive school system on much of the United Kingdom during the 1960's. Fortunately some grammar and secondary schools survived to provide an important measurement of the claims of the comprehensive school theorists. Such opportunities for the demonstration of State failure are rare – most ideologues are careful not to allow the existence of alternatives to "the truth"! In studies of examination results in grammar, secondary modern and comprehensive schools in 1983 and 1985 the National Council for Education Standards found that the 31,000 children at secondary modern and the 17,000 at grammar schools in the survey were achieving 30% to 40% more passes than those in comprehensives. The results were adjusted for differences in social class and covered 61 of the 104 local education authorities. Given these appalling discrepancies, what of the parents who wish to avoid the poor schools and send their children to the good schools? Will the compassionate State grant all parents a choice of school, through for instance the operation of a voucher system? Certainly not – such choice must remain the privilege of a more mobile middle class minority.

The irony of the comprehensive system, conceived to emancipate the less privileged – is that only the poorer classes really suffer. Formerly a grammar school was a place of excellence wherever it was situated, the size of its catchment area varying to reflect the absolute standard. But now a comprehensive school in Surrey is a far superior establishment to a comprehensive school in Durham and the middle class socialist who established them will know where to move to!

D. Regional Development. Most Government intervention is a superficial response to economic systems of which Government itself is usually the cause. Hundreds of millions of pounds are spent on Regional Devlopment Grants and there is a plethora of official agencies engaged – competitively – in "job creation". When Durham University recently organised a coordinating meeting for those agencies engaged in job creation and business support nearly 40 different groups appeared. They were unable even to agree on a central clearing and liaison system for better coordination of their efforts!

These regional agencies and grants are financed by withdrawing from those very regions billions of pounds in the form of individual and corporate taxation, national insurance contributions, road tax, etc. and non market pricing of gas, coal, electricity, water and telecommunications imposed and collected by a South East based bureaucracy. Note that, like all Government intervention, funds are extracted from businessmen who have created the wealth and then distributed by civil servants who have not.

In Wales and Scotland fully fledged "Development Agencies" are established to attract, invest and administer the massive inflow of public funds. The Welsh Development Agency published in its 1984/85 accounts a valuation of properties (mainly "advanced factories") of £313m. The national audit office described this valuation as an absurdity. Over a quarter of the agency's 1616 factory units were empty. An independent valuation by chartered surveyors put the value at £89.9m – a difference of £223m or 71%. The WDA argued that they had "a social role" so that "market criteria were not applicable".

What they mean of course is that, like all public sector operations, they wish to disguise the true cost of their "compassion" and enjoy their publically financed salaries without detailed scrutiny and accountability. In this case the discrepancy between image and reality was revealed in the only way it can be – by market pricing – but the danger in all public sector endeavour is that their burden on the rest of society cannot always be revealed. Even where it *can* theoretically be revealed, the absolute power of an ideological State can easily prevent such embarassing revelations.

E. State Factory Building. The Government-owned "English Industrial Estates Corporation" was established some 40 years ago to build factories and industrial premises. Once again it was assumed by the State that they knew more about factory building, location and industrial needs than those who habitually earned their living by doing such things.

149

In 1983 an Economist Intelligence Unit report on premises for small and medium sized businesses – the very businesses for which some Government "pump priming" of factory production may have been justified – found that the UK suffered from the worst provision of factories in Europe. To make matters worse, the survey found that of all the aspects of starting and expanding a business, the provision of premises was the most critical!

There is yet another serious aspect to the intervention of the State in factory building – apart that is from bankrupting those private sector companies engaged in such work through unfair subsidy. A small or growing business often has as its only real collateral for expansion capital in its factory. If the State is building factories "on spec" without any demonstrable need (or at such low rents and rates as to constitute a gift!) then the value of *all* factories falls. The small businessman therefore sees the value of his collateral and hence the prospects of a loan disappear.

F. A Council's Direct Labour Force. Local Councils have their own labour force to carry out road and housing repairs, refuse collection, etc. Until recently in the United Kingdom the efficiency of their operations could not be challenged since no other workforce could be given the opportunity to bid for that work. It was the usual story of lack of accountability among the "servants" of the people.

In 1985 Liverpool's 2,000 strong building and maintenance department was for the first time legally obliged to compete for the council contract but the Department's own Director said there was too much confusion to even submit a tender. Some workers had physically threatened him while he tried to carry through a £1m reorganisation of the department. The chaos was blamed on poor reporting systems and working methods and the union's habit of going direct to Labour Councillors behind the backs of management. The Director reported that "The resistance is to change and the fact that people have fairly easy earnings for very little work."

Such are the results of the politicisation of all aspects of social and economic life when we allow the arrogance of collectivism and the power of the State to override the responsible commercial initiatives of free individuals. Such is the power of the producer when politics controls rather than the responsibility of the market place when the consumer is sovereign.

G. Can the public authority control public authorities? A 1985 report by the Nature Conservancy Council on 138 sites of special scientific interest accused Government Departments such as the Forestry Commission, Ministry of Defence, water authorities, local councils and Crown Estates of causing damage which it described as "wilful".

H. Public Housing. The Department of the Environment has shown that council housing is not as popular with tenants, costs more and takes longer to build than private housing of similar quality. The Greater London Council's housing costs are 50% higher than private housing and the costs of Camden Council's housing is twice as high. The GLC has a ten year programme costing £10-£15m per annum to rectify defects in housing *built since 1964*. It is often maintained that the State can monitor and enforce quality standards better than the poor exploited consumer. But it is public sector housing and tower blocks which are uninhabitable and which have had to be demolished the length and breadth of the country.

As in education, if the people are given the power to choose, much of the "protective" bureaucracy of the State could be made redundant – but that of course is why it is not allowed!

CONCLUSION

The true definition of exploitation is the absence of any alternative for the exploited. The definition cannot for instance rest upon an arbitary statement of any particular level of power or reward. If many employees in a monopoly are poorly paid they may nevertheless be collectively *exploitive* of their fellow citzens (by imposing the total cost through the monopoly) rather than *exploited by* their employer. Others in relatively well paid jobs may, in relation to their value to society, still be exploited if their remuneration is the result of their employers power to exclude other employers who would pay them their (higher) market value.

This aspect of the *excluion of alternatives* lies also at the heart of the definition of collectivism. Naturally, collective initiatives are perfectly legitimate when people come together voluntarily in institutions, corporations and communities in order to achieve in groups what would not be achievable individually. There is always the ultimate check on these institutions in the form of free membership (you can leave a community or trade union and sell your company shares) free competition (there are other competing institutions) and freedom for others to consume or not consume the "collective" products. Collectivism however is a different matter. Here there is a strong element of certainty and determinism, of exclusion of competition and alternatives. Underlying such exclusive activity there is usually a pseudo scientific theory of absolute justice or "right" which, once having been defined, is challengable in reality. Collectivism is the assertion of truth and the collective coercion of *all* into the acceptance of that truth. Naturally such absolutism cannot arise so long as there is freedom of association and freedom of choice. Only one institution has the absolute power to prevent such freedom – the State, the ultimate collectivist from whose power and patronage subordinate collectivists derive *their* power.

The results are as we have noted in this book. If those are the results in the relatively open and liberal society of the United Kingdom we need not wonder at the combination of economic failure and political absolutism which characterise communist States. For in such societies all freedom of *expression,* never mind action, is denied – no voice, no vote, no visa to leave! That is the true definition of exploitation – of the people, by the State, for the Government.

PART IV

WHAT IS DEMOCRACY?

The principal characteristic of a Democracy is that it should express the will of the people. Perhaps more accurately it should express the *various* wills of the people. It is generally assumed that this is achieved through universal suffrage and Parliamentary representation and that it is through these political structures that the people "control" their own lives. It is also assumed that such political control is more just than the *purely* commercial process to which the people would otherwise be exposed.

Implicit in this scheme is a benevolent Government acting on behalf of the people who elect it. However, as we have seen, Government has taken on quite separate interests from those of the electrorate and is not averse to diverting resources from the people in order to sustain those interests. The notion of "Democracy" would therefore seem to warrant more critical analysis.

There are two basic forms of democratic control exercised by the people. That which accrues *indirectly* through the electoral vote and action on their behalf by an elected Government and that *direct* control over their own social and economic choices without reference to elected authority. In the natural course of events probably no more than 20% of the people's decisions need to be delegated to Government. The remainder of social activity is both more efficiently and more democratically effected by the spontaneity of direct public choice.

When Government and its agencies overstep the bounds of their "public good" roles and encroach upon the areas of free public choice, they contradict the democratic will. It does not take long for this contradiction to become apparent since Government is obliged to tax the populace either to finance public sector losses or to provide goods and services from the centre which the people would prefer to provide themselves. In order that this process of contradiction can be made more acceptable, it is disguised – by inflation. Inflation is such a pernicious and effective disguise that even politicians who administer the system are unaware of its effects. As the economy declines further, Government finds more and more

153

reasons for "social" intervention and its activities grow inexorably – not least in order to remedy the results of its previous interventions! Even those who were previously engaged in the commercial provision of goods and services to free consumers find that the offer of Government subsidy, grants and tax allowances (all of which subtly guide their decisions in politically acceptable directions) are too enticing to decline. Those who previously laboured to serve their fellow citizens then become part of the State Establishment which controls, contradicts and exploits those very citizens.

Direct public control declines as Government power increases. Those who have created wealth are taxed and the funds redistributed to those who have only consumed. Those who provide goods which the people buy are derided while those who waste the nation's resources in the production of goods which the people do not want are applauded as "socially responsible". High taxes destroy jobs and the revenue is distributed to the unemployed. Gas prices are subsidised and so are coal prices – the even handedness is at great cost to us all! Nuclear power is subsidised, so Government spends more on conservation to counteract the natural inclination to waste energy which is too cheap. Billions of pounds are extracted from the depressed regions of the United Kingdom in taxes and national insurance and then hundreds of millions are re-injected with maximum political profile. Income tax is raised but then £4,500m per annum is selectively handed back to those who enjoy mortgage interest relief. Tax relief on pensions encourages too many savings to be channelled towards institutional investors: the Business Expansion Scheme is therefore necessary to channel them back again. Protectionism and quotas on imports are effectively a tax on consumers and artificially raise the value of the currency, thus reducing exports. Government therefore spends more on export promotion.

The people, in the absence of Government intervention, would not engage in such circular pursuits. Government however finds the process rewarding: it requires considerable administration: larger offices and staff are justified as taxation and concomitant allowances and subsidies grow. Civil servants establish ever larger bureaucratic empires, each new face, desk or office justifying a more splendid title with more "appropriate" remuneration. This process of self aggrandisement reflects not so much the personal characteristics of civil servants or politicians but the natural result of uncontrolled, centralised *political* power.

Where indirect control by Government dominates at the expense of direct economic control through public choice the process is virtually irreversible, until, that is, we reach the point of social collapse and political revolution. In advanced and historically stable democracies a possible turning point is reached when it becomes increasingly difficult for Government to disguise the effects of high taxation and inflation. Stable revolutions were achieved in the UK in 1979 and in the United States in 1981 but even in those paragons of democratic stability there could be violent reactions against the attempts to re-establish public choice democracy. Certainly if monetary control is combined with a refusal to reform political institutions, "marketise" public monopolies and "disenfranchise" non-elected interest groups then the people will bear an even heavier and more unjust burden than under an inflationary regime. Social and economic tensions rise more quickly under a strict monetary regime as overt economic signals reveal that which covert political measures would have disguised.

An equally pernicious characteristic of political institutions is their ability to exclude alternatives. Their overriding universal power prevents stable conflict and gradual challenge to their particular, collectivist view of the truth. The direct democracy of public choice, however, principally realised through the market economy, naturally prevents any arbitrary hegemony of particular views, individuals or groups. There is a continuous challenge not only to established views and positions of power but also to material possessions. This democratic process under the Rule of Law and the public good roles of the minimal State ensure that the most powerful control exercised by the people is their ability to *choose*. The superficial control through their (indirect) ownership of State industry or Parliamentary legislation usually *reduces* their control.

The history of Government owned industry, particularly in the United Kingdom since 1945, has demonstrated that when Government *owns* industry *no-one* controls industry. The elimination of the private shareholder leads to the utter powerlessness of consumers and even conscientious producers. As usual when the Government sets out to protect and control it is the weak who suffer most. The car-less train traveller of modest means cannot by the simple exercise of choice exert pressure on high monopoly rail fares. The pensioner queuing for hours at the post office cannot take her custom elsewhere. The conscientious teacher sees no control by his pupils and their parents over his less qualified and less enthusiastic colleagues earning the same salary as he. The council house tenant in a poorly insulated house is powerless to affect the size of his heating bill: the council, not he, controls his house and he cannot move.

The role of the State is at its most pernicious when the direct interests of Government are at stake. When a company or individual is bankrupt his debts to the State (VAT, National Insurance contributions) must be paid first – other creditors must share what remains. If a soldier is injured in peacetime the armed services cannot by law be sued for negligence. Crown Immunity protects whole areas of Government activities from the possibility of persecution in those courts so readily utilised by Government against the people. A Minister, acting against the commercial advice of his advisers can commit, and lose, millions of pounds of public funds in the support of his political friends. A businessman who attempts the same with public money lent by a bank may be imprisoned for fraud. Pollution by a commercial company is the subject of court proceedings fines and even imprisonment while pollution by the State's industries is either not pursued in the courts or, if a fine is payable, it is a minor book keeping exercise to debit one Government account and credit another!

Governments of all colours are not slow to preach the gospel of public morality and personal responsibility. When it comes to their own activities they are the first in the queue for their "rights" and last in the queue for their responsibilities.

It is ironic that such aristocratic arrogance should characterise the institutions run by the most socialist of politicians. It is in the corridors of *political* power that noblesse oblige is dominant. It is in the party machines that cap doffing by the lower ranks and secrecy at the top prevent the open discussion of public issues. It is monopoly State control which emasculates the democracy of public choice. It is centralised macro-economic lever pulling which enhances the role of the academic economist and categorises consumers as a mindless and irresponsible "lumpenproletariat" to be stimulated and "fine tuned" at will.

Government has degenerated in all industrial democracies from its noble role as a delegated emancipator of the people to become an independent, voracious and unchallengeable institution increasingly remote from and contradictory of those who elect it. The process can only be reversed when the people begin to understand the democratic power of their non-political choices and see Government for what it is – a limited vehicle for actions which cannot be achieved by the people acting in free association.

As social decisions and choices are increasingly left to the people the resulting personal responsibility leads to more freedoms and less Government. Those who previously pulled economic levers, shuffled the vast files of impersonal bureaucracy and starred fixedly at symmetrical columns of Government statistics can return to the real world of public choice where the *actions* of the *people* provide the most stimulating and accurate reflection of society. It is odd that so many young idealists who leave University "to work with and for *people*"! then spend a lifetime writing reports compiled from second-hand statistics and struggling with administrative hierarchies run by people very much like themselves.

The release from those institutions into the more tangible world of the real actions and choices of market democracy forces the idealist to account not just to his own intellectual and social class but to all classes and all levels of education and intelligence. Not that there is a particularly strong correlation between class and education on the one hand and intelligence on the other. Many an upper middle class civil servant at home with national expenditure accounts would be lost running a corner sweet shop. An academic would not survive the rigours of market democracy as well as a production line worker. Indeed it is the awareness of these unfavourable comparisons which reinforces much middle class defence of the more "ordered" activities of State patronage!

There will always be important public good roles for Government – although they will naturally diminish as economic progress and political sophistication permit ever wider areas for public choice and personal responsibility. Public goods are as natural as commercial activity in the service of the people. But, like commercial activity, Government must justify its role, not just in periodic elections of political parties each taking its turn at the same levers of State power, but continuously by expanding the areas of direct democracy and confining its own activities to emancipating the people to take on the power to choose.

Where the definition of Democracy is limited to Parliamentary elections the State's commands replace the public choice. Where Democracy means public choice, expressed principally through non political means, then Government remains true to its original and only justification – the *service* of the people.

ACKNOWLEDGEMENTS

"Inflation and the Oil Price" is based on an article published in the Financial Times "Energy Economist" in March 1984

"Inflation and Middle Class Values" was published in The Salisbury Review in October 1984

"Incomes Policies do not work" was published in the Journal of Economic Affairs in April 1982

"Making Monetarism Work" was a Bow Group Paper published in October 1981

"Edward Heath and the People of Consett" was published in the Journal of Economic Affairs in October 1985

"Income Wealth and Capital Taxation" was published by the Adam Smith Institute in March 1985

"Overseas Aid by Foreign Trade" was published in the Journal of Economic Affairs in January 1982

"A Safer Road for 'Young Nation' Debtors" was published in Crossbow, Spring 1985

"The Moral Basis of Monetarism" was a pamphlet published by Compuprint Publishing in January 1984 ISBN 0 9509353 0 1

GOVERNMENT AGAINST THE PEOPLE

The author is concerned with the gross discrepancy between the theory of Democracy as the expression of the people's will and the practice of "Democratic Government" which has been based on the contradiction of that will. A change of political hand at the levers of State control does nothing to reduce the number of those levers. The Establishments of Left and Right – so brilliantly combined in post war corporatism – are increasingly seen as two forms of the same authoritarianism.

For those politicians who still claim that the first step in the people's salvation is the Government's intervention, the sad tale of Government failure contained in these pages may induce a long overdue modesty.

> "The all powerful State soon earns the contempt of those it set out to protect and the friendship of those it set out to control."
>
> "Crown immunity protects whole areas of State activity from prosecution in those courts so readily utilised by Government against the people."
>
> "The people of Clyde, Tyne and Mersey are now but ideological cannon fodder in the vaccuous rhetoric of politicians on their ambitious road (South) to Westminster."
>
> "Tax thresholds and tax rates are "socially" set at levels which miraculousy avoid the wealth enjoyed by the average Cabinet Minister."
>
> "The European Common Market is not common nor European nor a market. It may be the apotheosis of Government but it represents the nadir of Democracy."
>
> "Whereas most Parliaments only relapse into institutionalised horse-trading after some attempt has been made to represent electors, the European Parliament was not so tardy."
>
> "It is the actions and choices of *market* democracy which force the middle class idealist to account not just to his own intellectual and social class but to all classes and all levels of education and intelligence."
>
> "The only solution to the control of the State is the freedom of the people to choose – but that threatens some very comfortable, not to say profitable myths about "Democracy.""

Comments on Rodney Atkinson's work:

"Excellent" (Nobel Laureate Milton Friedman) "Very good indeed" (Rt Hon David Howell MP) "Brilliantly argued" (Financial Times Energy Economist) "Fascinating" (Milton Friedman) "I read it with great pleasure" (Professor Mancur Olson, author The Rise and Decline of Nations).